My
Apple Watch™

SECOND EDITION

Craig James Johnston

que®

My Apple Watch™ Second Edition

Copyright © 2016 by Pearson Education, Inc.

ISBN-13: 978-0-7897-5662-6
ISBN-10: 0-7897-5662-5

Costco Edition ISBN 13: 978-0-7897-5825-5
Costco Edition ISBN 10: 0-7897-5825-3

Library of Congress Control Number: 2015953093

Printed in the United States of America

First Printing: November 2015

Trademarks

All terms mentioned in this book that are known to be trademarks or service marks have been appropriately capitalized. Que Publishing cannot attest to the accuracy of this information. Use of a term in this book should not be regarded as affecting the validity of any trademark or service mark.

Apple Watch is a trademark of Apple Inc., registered in the U.S. and other countries.

Warning and Disclaimer

Every effort has been made to make this book as complete and as accurate as possible, but no warranty or fitness is implied. The information provided is on an "as is" basis. The author and the publisher shall have neither liability nor responsibility to any person or entity with respect to any loss or damages arising from the information contained in this book.

Special Sales

For information about buying this title in bulk quantities, or for special sales opportunities (which may include electronic versions; custom cover designs; and content particular to your business, training goals, marketing focus, or branding interests), please contact our corporate sales department at corpsales@pearsoned.com or (800) 382-3419.

For government sales inquiries, please contact governmentsales@pearsoned.com.

For questions about sales outside the U.S., please contact international@pearsoned.com.

Editor-in-Chief
Greg Wiegand

Senior Acquisitions Editor
Laura Norman

Senior Development Editor
Laura Norman

Managing Editor
Sandra Schroeder

Project Editor
Mandie Frank

Copy Editor
Bart Reed

Indexer
Erika Millen

Proofreader
Debbie Williams

Technical Editor
Paul Sihvonen-Binder

Editorial Assistant
Kristen Watterson

Designer
Mark Shirar

Compositor
Studio Galou

Contents at a Glance

Prologue	Getting to Know Your Apple Watch	3
Chapter 1	Personalizing Your Watch	29
Chapter 2	Messages, Email, and Phone Calls	105
Chapter 3	Using Siri	137
Chapter 4	Using Apple Maps	149
Chapter 5	Playing Music	165
Chapter 6	Using Apple Pay	187
Chapter 7	Using Your Watch to Stay Active	195
Chapter 8	Installing and Managing Watch Apps	211
Chapter 9	Using Other Watch Apps	221
Chapter 10	Useful Watch Apps	235
Index		251

Table of Contents

Prologue   Getting to Know Your Apple Watch   3

Your Apple Watch's External Features 3

    Front and Right Side 4

    Back 5

First-Time Setup 6

Learning How to Use Your Apple Watch 15

    Use the Digital Crown 15

    Use the Side Button 17

    Use the Touchscreen 18

    Use the Lock Screen 19

Interacting with the Watch Face 20

    Work with Notifications 21

    Use Glances 23

    Run an App 24

    Quickly Access Your Friends 25

    Command Your Watch Using Siri 26

1   Personalizing Your Apple Watch   29

Choosing and Customizing Your Watch Face 29

    Choose a New Watch Face 30

    Customize an Existing Watch Face 31

    Create a New Version of an Existing Watch Face 36

    Delete a Watch Face 38

Using the Photo Album and Photo Watch Faces 40

    Synchronize a Photo Album 41

    Change Overall Watch Face Functionality 49

Rearranging App Icons and Activating Airplane Mode 52

    Move App Icons 52

    Configure Do Not Disturb 53

    Coordinate Airplane Mode 58

Managing Glances 61

    Rearranging Glances 61

    Add Glances 63

Configuring General Watch Settings 65

    Change General Settings 66

    Add Accessibility 69

Changing Screen, Sound, and Haptics Settings 72

    Adjust Brightness and Text Size 72

    Adjust Sounds and Haptics 73

    Control Notifications 76

Changing Passcode-Related Settings 78

Configuring Motion and Fitness Privacy Settings 80

Changing Settings for Built-in Watch Apps 82

    Activity 82

    Calendar 85

    Clock 86

    Contacts 88

    Friends 89

    Mail 90

    Maps 92

    Messages 92

    Music 94

    Wallet and Apple Pay 95

    Phone 96

    Photos 98

    Stocks 99

    Weather 100

    Workout 101

Change Settings for Third-Party Watch Apps 102

2   Messages, Emails, and Phone Calls   105

Working with Messages 105

    Read and Respond to Messages from Notifications 106

    Read and Respond to Messages from the
        Messages App 110

    Compose a New Message from the Messages App 112

    Compose a New Message from the Friends List 115

Using Digital Touch 117

    Send a Digital Touch 118

    Receive a Digital Touch 120

Working with Email 121

    Read Email from Within a Notification 121

    Reply To Email from Within a Notification 122

    Dictate Your Response 123

    Respond Using an Emoji 124

    Use the Mail App 126

Make and Receive Phone Calls 128

    Handle an Incoming Call 128

    Options During a Call 130

    Use the Phone App 130

    Use Your Favorites 131

    Manage Recent Calls 131

    Place a Call from Your Contacts 132

    Manage Voicemail 133

3 Using Siri 137

Activating Siri 137

    Raise Your Wrist 138

    Press the Digital Crown 138

Using Siri 139

    Time-Related Requests 139

    Informational Requests 143

4 Using Apple Maps 149

Launching Maps 150

    Search for a Place and Get Directions to It 151

    Hand Off Directions Between Your iPhone and Watch 154

    Stick a Pin in the Map 155

    Get Directions to One of Your Contacts 156

    View Information About a Landmark 158

Get Transit Directions 158

5 Playing Music 165

Finding and Playing Music 166

    My Music 167

Controlling Playback 175

Use the Playback Controls to Play, Pause, and
Jump to Other Songs 175

Use Additional Playback Controls to Repeat, Shuffle,
and Play Music on Other Devices 176

Playing Music from Your Apple Watch 177

Creating a Playlist on Your iPhone 177

Synchronize a Playlist to Your Watch 179

Pair a Bluetooth Device 181

Play a Playlist on Your Watch 182

6   Using Apple Pay   187

Adding Cards to Apple Pay 187

Pay with your Watch 192

7   Using Your Watch to Stay Active   195

Becoming Familiar with the Activity App 196

Navigate the Activity App on Your Watch 196

Change Your Move Goal 198

Use the Activity App on your iPhone 199

Using the Workout App 200

Choose a Type of Workout and Start Your Workout ... 201

View Information and End Your Workout 202

Using the Health App 203

Choose Health Sources 205

View the Health Data 207

8   Installing and Managing Watch Apps   211

Finding Watch Apps 212

Installing Watch Apps 213

Managing Your Watch Apps 214

Choose Watch Apps to Install or Uninstall 214

Rearrange App Icons 215

Decide Whether Apps Should Automatically Install ... 216

Change App Notification Settings 216

9   Using Other Watch Apps   221

Using Media-Related Apps 221

Control Your Apple TV or Mac 222

Control Pandora 224

Control Your iPhone's Camera 225

Using Social Media Apps 226

Using Instagram 226

Using Twitter 227

Using Time- and Date-Related Apps 228

Start a Timer 228

Use the Stopwatch 229

See the Time Around the World 229

Managing Alarms 230

See the Weather Around the World 232

Check on Your Schedule 233

10   Useful Watch Apps   235

Calling an Uber Car 236

Calculating the Tip Using Calcbot 237

Finding a Starbucks and Checking Your Rewards 239

Translating Your Words 240

Working with Email Using Outlook 243

Read Email As It Arrives 244

Read Emails From the Outlook App 245

Using Evernote 247

Controlling Your PowerPoint Presentation 249

Index   251

About the Author

Craig James Johnston has been involved with technology since his high school days at Glenwood High in Durban, South Africa, when his school was given some Apple][Europluses. From that moment, technology captivated him, and he has owned, supported, evangelized, and written about it.

Craig has been involved in designing and supporting large-scale enterprise networks with integrated email and directory services since 1989. He has held many different IT-related positions in his career, ranging from sales support engineer to mobile architect for a 40,000-smartphone infrastructure at a large bank.

In addition to designing and supporting mobile computing environments, Craig cohosts the CrackBerry.com podcast as well as guest hosting on other podcasts, including iPhone and iPad Live podcasts. You can see Craig's previously published work in his books *Professional BlackBerry*, *My iMovie*, and many books in the *My* series covering devices by BlackBerry, Palm, HTC, Motorola, Samsung, and Google.

Craig also enjoys high-horsepower, high-speed vehicles and tries very hard to keep to the speed limit while driving them.

Originally from Durban, South Africa, Craig has lived in the United Kingdom, the San Francisco Bay Area, and New Jersey, where he now lives with his wife, Karen, and a couple of cats.

Craig would love to hear from you. Feel free to contact Craig about your experiences with *My Apple Watch* at http://www.CraigsBooks.info.

All comments, suggestions, and feedback are welcome, including positive and negative.

Dedication

I love deadlines. I like the whooshing sound they make as they fly by.
—Douglas Adams

Acknowledgments

I would like to express my deepest gratitude to the following people on the *My Apple Watch* team, who all worked extremely hard on this book:

- Laura Norman, senior acquisitions editor, who worked with me to give this project an edge.

- Paul Sihvonen-Binder, technical editor, who double-checked to ensure the technical accuracy of this book.

- Laura Norman, who also developed the manuscript skillfully.

- Bart Reed, who edited the manuscript with a light touch.

- Mandie Frank, who kept the book project on schedule.

- Louisa Adair, who combined the text and art into colorful pages.

We Want to Hear from You!

As the reader of this book, *you* are our most important critic and commentator. We value your opinion and want to know what we're doing right, what we could do better, what areas you'd like to see us publish in, and any other words of wisdom you're willing to pass our way.

We welcome your comments. You can email or write to let us know what you did or didn't like about this book—as well as what we can do to make our books better.

Please note that we cannot help you with technical problems related to the topic of this book.

When you write, please be sure to include this book's title and author as well as your name and email address. We will carefully review your comments and share them with the author and editors who worked on the book.

Email: feedback@quepublishing.com

Mail: Que Publishing
         ATTN: Reader Feedback
         800 East 96th Street
         Indianapolis, IN 46240 USA

Reader Services

Visit our website and register this book at quepublishing.com/register for convenient access to any updates, downloads, or errata that might be available for this book.

In this prologue, you become familiar with the external features of the Apple Watch and the basics of getting started. Topics include the following:

→ Getting to know your Apple Watch's external features
→ Setting up your Apple Watch for the first time
→ Learning how to interact with your Apple Watch

Prologue

Getting to Know Your Apple Watch

Let's start by getting to know more about your Apple Watch by examining the external features, device features, and how you will interact with your Apple Watch.

Your Apple Watch's External Features

Becoming familiar with the external features of your Apple Watch is a good place to start because you will be using them often. This section covers some of the technical specifications of your Apple Watch, including the touchscreen.

Front and Right Side

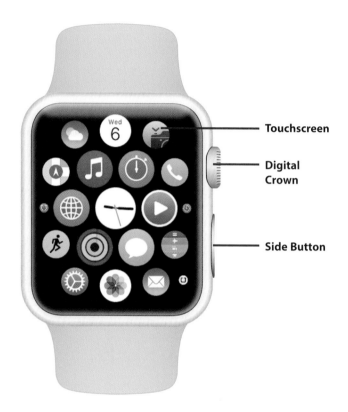

Touchscreen

Digital Crown

Side Button

- **Touchscreen**—The Apple Watch comes in two screen sizes: 38mm and 42mm. The 38mm screen has a resolution of 340×272 pixels, whereas the 42mm screen has a resolution of 390×312 pixels. The screen incorporates capacitive touch, which allows you to use your finger to make gestures to control the Watch.

- **Digital Crown**—The Digital Crown is very similar to a regular mechanical watch Crown. Like a mechanical watch Crown, the Digital Crown can be rotated between your thumb and forefinger, or by running your finger over the edge of the Crown. You can press the Digital Crown to see the Home Screen, showing icons representing all apps installed on your Watch, similar to pressing the Home button on your iPhone. You can press and hold the Digital Crown to activate Siri, and you can double-press the Crown to return to the last Watch app you were using.

- **Side Button**—Press the Side Button to see and interact with your friends. Double-press the Side Button to activate Apple Pay. Press and hold the Side Button to choose whether you want to power off your Watch, activate Power Reserve, or lock your Watch.

Back

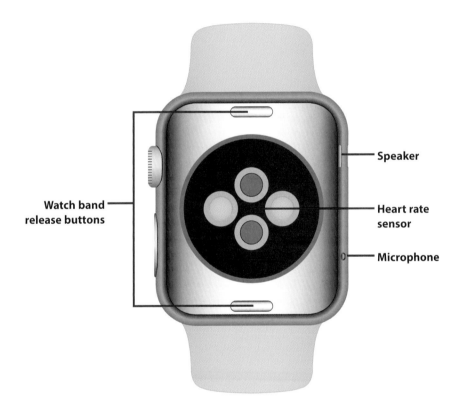

Watch band release buttons

Speaker

Heart rate sensor

Microphone

- **Watch band release buttons**—Press to release the band from your Watch and replace it with a new one.

- **Microphone**—You use the microphone when you are on a phone call, or to speak commands to Siri.

- **Speaker**—The speaker is used while you're on a phone call, and it is also used to play all audio, including notifications and music.

- **Heart rate sensor**—The heart rate sensor uses infrared and green light to measure your heart rate. Your Watch captures your heart rate automatically every 10 minutes.

First-Time Setup

Your Apple Watch only works when it is paired with your iPhone. You must be using an iPhone 5 or later; otherwise, you will not be able to use your Apple Watch. Finally, your iPhone must be running iOS version 8.2 or later.

1. Put your Apple Watch on your wrist.

2. Press and hold the Side Button until you see the Apple logo.

3. Use the Digital Crown to choose your language, and tap the language on the screen to select it.

4. Your Apple Watch now pairs with your iPhone. Leave your Apple Watch on your wrist, and pick up your iPhone to continue the steps.

5. Tap the Apple Watch app to open it.

What If I Don't See the Apple Watch App?

The Apple Watch app is included with iOS 8.2 or later. If you don't see the Apple Watch app on your iPhone, it is most likely because you have not yet updated to iOS 8.2. To do this, tap the Settings icon, tap General, and tap Software Update. You may need to free up some space on your iPhone to accommodate the update.

6. Tap the My Watch icon.

7. Tap Start Pairing.

8. Hold your iPhone so that your Apple Watch fits into the viewfinder. Your Apple Watch's screen displays colorful patterns, and your iPhone uses those patterns to complete the Bluetooth pairing between your iPhone and Apple Watch.

9. Tap Set Up Apple Watch once you see the next screen.

10. Tap Left or Right to choose on which wrist you will be wearing your Apple Watch.

Having a Better Right Wrist Experience

Your choice of which wrist you wear your Apple Watch (left or right) helps the Apple Watch more accurately determine when you are lifting your arm. If you wear your Apple Watch on your right wrist, like wearing a mechanical watch on your right wrist, nothing about the Watch will change. If you find it is awkward to manipulate the Digital Crown and Side Button, you have an additional setting that allows you to wear the Watch upside down so that the Digital Crown and Side Button are now on the left of the Watch. This may allow you to manipulate the Digital Crown and Side Button more easily. This setting also flips the onscreen image upside down so it appears right side up to you. To make this change, after you have finished setting up your Watch, in the Apple Watch app, tap General, tap Watch Orientation, and tap Digital Crown on Left Side.

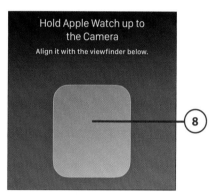

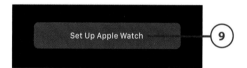

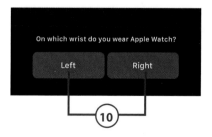

11. Tap Agree to agree with the terms and conditions of using your Apple Watch.

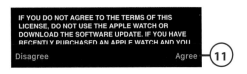

IF YOU DO NOT AGREE TO THE TERMS OF THIS LICENSE, DO NOT USE THE APPLE WATCH OR DOWNLOAD THE SOFTWARE UPDATE. IF YOU HAVE RECENTLY PURCHASED AN APPLE WATCH AND YOU

Disagree   Agree — (11)

12. Tap Agree again to confirm that you agree with the terms and conditions.

13. Type the password for your Apple ID.

14. Tap Next.

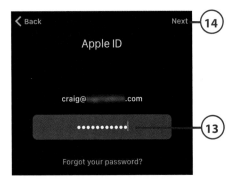

Terms and Conditions

I agree to the Apple Watch OS Terms and Conditions and the Apple Privacy Policy.

Cancel | Agree — (12)

15. Tap OK on the Location Services screen to continue. If you have Location Services turned off on your iPhone, you are asked if you want to enable it on this screen.

< Back   Next — (14)

Apple ID

craig@⬛⬛⬛.com

•••••••••••• — (13)

Forgot your password?

Why Do I Need Location Services?

Your iPhone and Apple Watch can use your current location to provide important information, such as the weather in your current location, adjust the time correctly based on the time zone you are in, and provide walking or driving directions. If you keep Location Services turned off, you will not be able to take advantage of many of the Apple Watch's features.

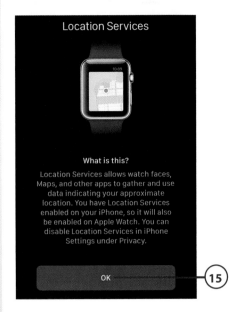

Location Services

What is this?

Location Services allows watch faces, Maps, and other apps to gather and use data indicating your approximate location. You have Location Services enabled on your iPhone, so it will also be enabled on Apple Watch. You can disable Location Services in iPhone Settings under Privacy.

OK — (15)

16. Tap OK on the Siri screen to continue with setup. If you have Siri turned off on your iPhone, you are asked if you want to enable it on this screen.

Why Do I Need Siri?

Your iPhone and Apple Watch can listen for your voice commands to send messages, place calls, create calendar events, launch apps, and more. With Siri enabled, you are able to lift your wrist and say "Hey Siri," followed by commands.

17. Tap OK on the Diagnostics screen to continue. If you have the option to send usage and diagnostics information to Apple turned off on your iPhone, you are asked whether you want to enable it on this screen.

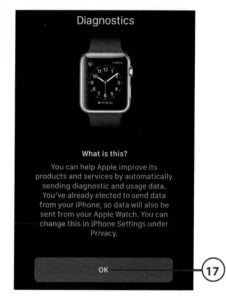

18. Tap Create a Passcode to enter a four-digit passcode on your Watch. The passcode is used in the future to unlock your Watch when you take it off and then put it back on.

19. Enter a passcode on your Apple Watch (not shown). After you have entered your new passcode, keep looking at your Watch for the next step. If you chose not to add a passcode, skip to step 21.

Apple Watch Passcode

Create a Passcode — (18)

Add a Long Passcode

What is this?

When you set a passcode, Apple Watch locks when you take it off and requires the passcode to unlock. This helps protect your data.

Don't Add Passcode

Create a long passcode that must be entered on your iPhone

Skip the passcode step

How Does the Passcode Work?

Your Apple Watch uses a sensor on the back to detect when it is in contact with your skin, so it knows whether or not it is being worn. If you set a four-digit passcode in step 18, when you remove your Watch, it will lock itself. When you put your Watch back on, it will prompt you to enter the passcode before you are able to use it. You enter the four-digit passcode on your Watch. If you chose to create a long passcode, when you put your Watch on, you are prompted to enter that longer passcode on your iPhone before your Watch is unlocked. Remember that you only need to unlock your Watch if you take it off and later put it back on. It is advisable to use a passcode on your Watch because if you lose it, or it is stolen, your information will be vulnerable. What makes securing your Watch with a passcode more manageable is that you can choose to have your Watch unlocked when you unlock your iPhone (see step 20). With this option enabled, if your Watch detects that it is on your wrist, and you unlock your iPhone, your Watch automatically unlocks itself. Finally, if you choose not to add a passcode to your Watch, you are unable to use Apple Pay from your Watch.

20. Choose whether you want your Apple Watch to be unlocked when it is on your wrist and you unlock your iPhone.

21. Tap Install All to install any Watch apps.

How Do I Already Have Watch Apps?

Apps already installed on your iPhone might include a Watch version of those apps. Now that you have your Watch, you can take advantage of those additional Watch apps. An example of this is the Twitter Watch app, which allows you to quickly access your timeline or see the top trends.

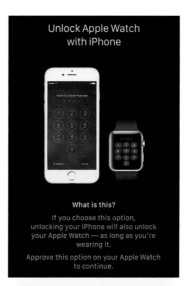

Don't install any Watch apps right now

Twitter Watch app

22. Your Watch synchronizes with your iPhone for the first time. You can either wait on this screen, or press the Home button on your iPhone (not shown) to continue working and wait for an alert from the Apple Watch app letting you know that the synchronization is complete.

23. Tap OK on your iPhone when you see the information message telling you that your Apple ID has been used to sign in to your Apple Watch. This is just confirming what you did in step 13.

24. Tap OK, and look at your Watch for the remaining steps of the Watch setup. If your Watch has gone to sleep, press the Digital Crown to wake it up and continue to step 25.

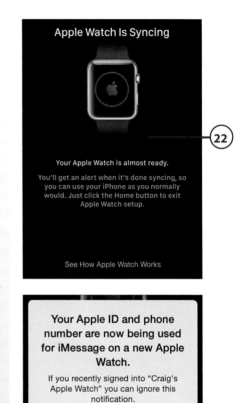

25. Tap Set Up the Activity App and then swipe through the screens that explain how your activity is tracked.

26. Tap Get Started to choose your daily activity level and how many calories you want to burn each day.

27. Tap to choose how active you are during the day. The choices you make tell the Activity app how many calories you normally burn each day, but you have the option of adjusting that in the next step.

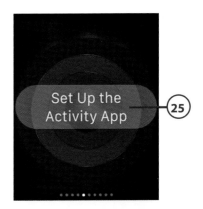

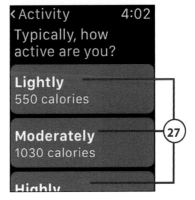

28. Tap the minus and plus symbols to decrease or increase the number of calories you want to burn each day, also known as your Move Goal.

29. Tap Start Moving.

30. Press the Digital Crown to see a list of your Watch apps when you see the Activity screen. At this point your Apple Watch is completely set up.

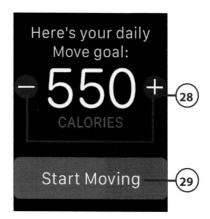

Wait for Apps to Finish Installing

After you finish setting up your Apple Watch, you will naturally want to start exploring it right away. If you chose to install all Apple Watch apps in step 21, those apps might still be installing and might slow down your Watch. You can see the progress of an app install because it looks very much like the app install progress icon you see on your iPhone. Either wait for all apps to finish installing or be aware that you may experience some delayed responses from your Watch as they install.

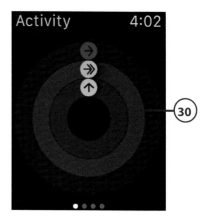

Watch app install progress

Learning How to Use Your Apple Watch

Your Apple Watch is designed to allow you to quickly view and respond to alerts, perform simple tasks, run apps, communicate with friends, and of course show you the time. This section covers the essential information you need to use your Apple Watch.

You'll need to master a few touchscreen gestures and button interactions in order to interact with your Watch more efficiently. Let's take a look at them.

Use the Digital Crown

The Digital Crown is modeled after the Crown on a mechanical watch, and can be turned by using your thumb and forefinger or by rolling it under your forefinger. You can also press the Digital Crown, double-press it, or press and hold it to achieve certain actions.

1. Press the Digital Crown to toggle between the time and the Home Screen that shows the list of apps. For example, if you are looking at the list of apps and you press the Digital Crown, you see the time using the watch face you previously chose to use. If you are looking at your watch face and you press the Digital Crown, you are taken to the list of apps.

2. Press the Digital Crown to return to the centermost app when viewing the list of apps. For example, if you have been scrolling around the list of apps and want to quickly return to the centermost app (the clock), press the Digital Crown.

3. Press the Digital Crown to exit an app and return to the Home Screen.

4. Double-press the Digital Crown to switch to the app you were last using. For example, if you were looking at your email in the Mail app, and then switched to the Photos app, double-press the Digital Crown to switch back to the Mail app.

5. Press and hold the Digital Crown for two seconds to activate Siri. After you feel the tap on your wrist, you can speak commands to Siri, or ask her questions.

6. Rotate the Digital Crown to scroll up and down a list. Any time an app presents you with a list, such as a list of your email or list of songs, you can scroll through that list using the Digital Crown. As you turn the Digital Crown, an indicator shows you how far down the list you are. You can also use the Digital Crown to move through options in an app. For example, when you are customizing your watch face, you can scroll through the customization options using the Digital Crown.

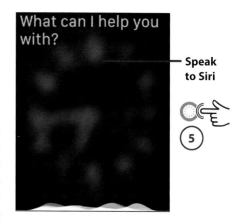

Speak to Siri

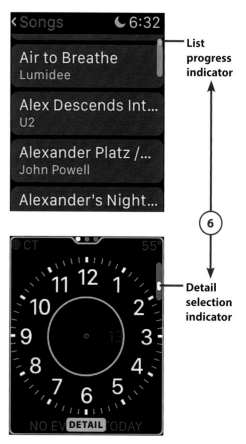

List progress indicator

Detail selection indicator

Use the Side Button

You can also press the Side Button, double-press it, or press and hold it to achieve certain actions.

1. Press the Side Button once to see your Friends list and access ways to interact with them.

2. Double-press the Side Button to activate Apple Pay. Once Apple Pay is activated, hold your Watch near the reader at the checkout counter to pay for items.

3. Press and hold the Side Button for two seconds to choose whether you want to power off your Apple Watch, activate Power Reserve, or lock your Apple Watch by swiping one of the choices to the right.

What Is Power Reserve?

When your Watch is in Power Reserve mode, it just shows the time. Your Watch stops communicating with your iPhone, and you are not able to use any of your Watch apps. Power Reserve mode is automatically enabled when your Watch battery is getting low on power, so you shouldn't need to activate it manually. To exit Power Reserve mode, first charge your Watch, and then press and hold the Side Button until you see the Apple logo. This indicates that your Watch is restarting.

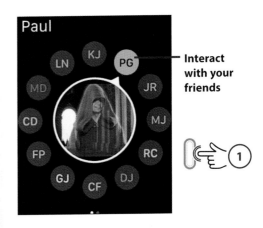

Interact with your friends

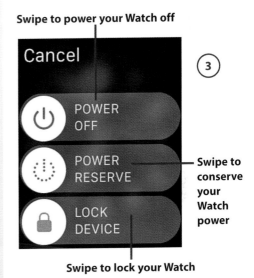

Swipe to power your Watch off

Swipe to conserve your Watch power

Swipe to lock your Watch

Use the Touchscreen

In addition to using the Digital Crown and Side Button, you also interact with your Apple Watch by touching the screen, which is known as making gestures on the screen. You can tap, double-tap, swipe, and Force Touch.

- **Tap**—To start an app, tap its icon. Tap an onscreen button to select it. Tap the numbers of the onscreen keypad to unlock your Watch.

- **Swipe**—Swipe in any direction on the screen. You can swipe slowly or quickly. Swipe a notification to clear it. Swipe to explore your photos.

- **Drag**—Dragging is essentially a swipe, but with this gesture you drag an onscreen object to perform a function. Drag the map in the Maps app to reposition it. Drag the slider left to right to power off your Watch.

- **Double-tap**—Double-tapping is like double-clicking a mouse on a desktop computer. Tap the screen twice in quick succession. For example, you can double-tap the map in the Maps app to zoom in.

- **Force Touch**—Force Touch is a hard press on the screen. When you perform a Force Touch, you will see options to choose that are contextual. For example, if you Force Touch on a watch face, you can customize it or choose a different watch face. If you Force Touch during a workout, you can stop the workout.

Practicing Force Touch

The best way to practice how hard you need to press the screen to use the Force Touch gesture is to practice Force Touch on a watch face. Start by pressing softly, and you will notice that the watch face starts zooming out very slowly. The harder you push, the further it zooms out, until you eventually see the word Customize appear below the watch face, and feel a tap on your wrist (and your finger). Tap the watch face to zoom in on it again. Now, press on the screen again, but use the same amount of force that you were using when you saw the word Customize appear and felt the tap on your wrist and finger. If you got the pressure correct, you should immediately see the word Customize appear and feel the tap on your wrist. Use this same amount of pressure in the future when you want to perform the Force Touch gesture to access additional features, such as choosing the view mode for the Calendar app.

Use the Lock Screen

If you chose to lock your Watch with a passcode (highly recommended), when you take your Watch off, it locks itself. When you put your Watch back on your wrist, it remains locked until you unlock it. Once your Watch is unlocked, it remains unlocked until you take it off, or your choose to manually lock it.

Indicates Watch is locked

1. Remove your Watch and wait for it to lock. Replace it on your wrist and lift your wrist to interact with your Watch in any way, such as by tapping the screen to access the Enter Passcode screen. Alternatively, just wait a few seconds after raising your wrist, and the Enter Passcode screen appears automatically.

2. Enter the four-digit passcode to unlock your Watch.

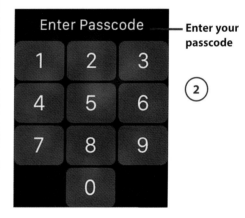

Enter your passcode

Other Unlock Methods

When you set up your Watch, you might have chosen to use a long passcode. If you did, instead of your Watch prompting you to enter the passcode, your iPhone prompts you to enter the long passcode. If you chose to have your Watch automatically unlocked when you unlock your iPhone, simply unlock your iPhone using a passcode or Touch ID, and your Watch is also unlocked. If you are holding the Watch in your hand, you can still unlock it by entering the passcode. Because it is not on your wrist, your Watch does not automatically unlock when you unlock your iPhone because it cannot detect your skin.

Interacting with the Watch Face

The most common screen you see on your Watch is the watch face. Here is how to interact with the various watch faces. Depending on the watch face you choose, and how you customize it, it might include one or more *complications*, which are additional icons that show information but also sometimes allow you to tap them to open the associated app. We will cover choosing and customizing your watch face in more depth in Chapter 1, "Personalizing Your Apple Watch."

What Are Complications?

Makers of mechanical watches use the term "complications" to describe any mechanical watch function that is in addition to displaying the time in hours and minutes. In fact, a watch that only shows the hours and minutes is said to have a simple movement. Because mechanical watches are made using tiny gears, springs, and other mechanical pieces, adding extra functionality is complicated, and hence adding something such as the date to the display is said to be a complication. This is true not only in watch construction, but also when the watch needs to be repaired. Some examples of mechanical watch complications include a chronograph, moon phases, and displaying time in different times zones. When Apple designed the Apple Watch, they wanted to keep the traditional language surrounding watches, and so a watch face on your Apple Watch can include complications, which are essentially icons that show additional information such as the time in a different time zone or the weather.

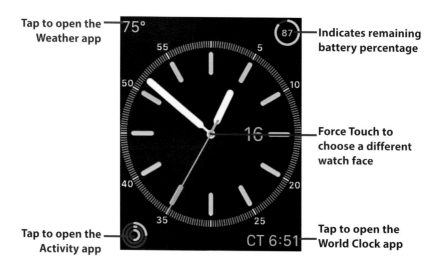

Work with Notifications

When an app needs to alert you, your Watch taps you on the wrist. If you lift your arm within a second or two after you feel the tap, the notification is displayed on the screen. You are then able to dismiss it, or in some cases, take action on it. For example, if someone sends you a text message (or iMessage), you can reply to that message right on your Watch. More on choosing which notifications you want to see on your Apple Watch can be found in Chapter 1.

If you ignore the notification, later when you look at your Watch you will see a red dot on the top of your Watch screen. This indicates that you have missed notifications. Swipe down from the top of the Watch screen to see and manage your notifications.

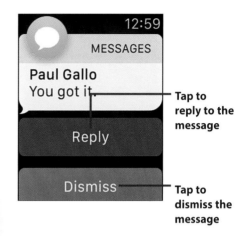

Tap to reply to the message

Tap to dismiss the message

Swipe down to see the notifications

Indicates that there are missed notifications

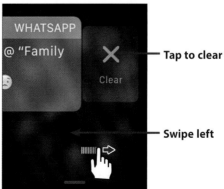

Tap to clear

Swipe left

To clear notifications one by one, swipe the notification to the left and then tap the Clear icon. To clear all notifications at the same time, Force Touch and tap the Clear All icon.

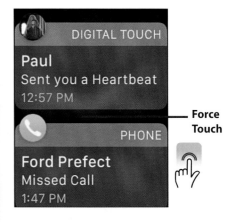

Force Touch

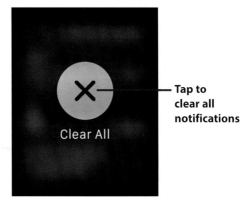

Tap to clear all notifications

Use Glances

Glances are similar to Widgets on your iPhone. They provide real-time information and some functionality. Examples of Glances are Calendar Glance, Weather Glance, and even the Settings Glance. Besides the built-in Glances, certain apps you install on your Watch may include their own Glances. Examples of these include the Instagram app and the Swarm app. Swipe up from the bottom of your Watch screen to see Glances. Swipe left and right to scroll through the Glances. We will cover more on choosing which Glances you want to see on your Apple Watch in Chapter 1.

Swipe up to see Glances

Swipe left and right to move between Glances

Run an App

In addition to telling the time, allowing you to respond to notifications, and showing you information via Glances, your Apple Watch can run apps. To run an app, press the Digital Crown to view the available apps, and then tap an app icon. Turning the Digital Crown zooms in and out of the list of apps. More on choosing which apps you want to see on your Apple Watch and how the list of apps is laid out can be found in Chapter 1.

If you don't see the app icon, swipe around on the screen to move the view of apps to find the one you are looking for. Pressing the Digital Crown exits the list of apps and returns to the watch face.

If you zoom in all the way to an app icon at the center of your Watch screen, that particular app launches.

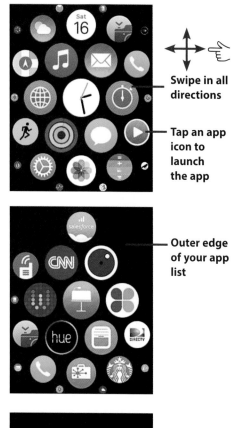

Swipe in all directions

Tap an app icon to launch the app

Outer edge of your app list

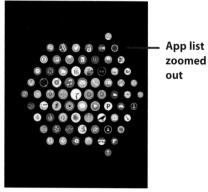

App list zoomed out

Quickly Access Your Friends

If you press the Side Button, you see the Friends list (contacts are called Friends in the Watch app). Turning the Digital Crown allows you to choose a friend. If you wait a few seconds after selecting your friend, you see a screen of communication options. You can find more on choosing which friends you want to see on your Apple Watch in Chapter 1.

For friends that do not have Apple Watches, you can call them and send them text messages (and iMessages). For friends that do have Apple Watches, you can also communicate with them using Digital Touch. Digital Touch allows you to send your actual heart beat, send pictures you draw on your Watch screen, and send a sequence of taps. See Chapter 2, "Messages, Email, and Phone Calls," for more on interacting with the Friends app.

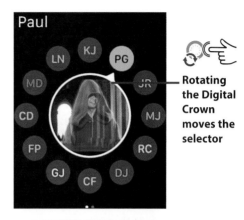

Rotating the Digital Crown moves the selector

Friend without an Apple Watch

Tap to call   **Tap to send a message**

Friend with an Apple Watch

Tap to send a message

Tap to call   **Tap to use Digital Touch**

Command Your Watch Using Siri

If you raise your wrist and say, "Hey Siri," Siri starts listening for your spoken commands. You can also press and hold the Digital Crown to activate Siri. Some examples of using Siri are "Hey Siri, where can I get a pizza around here?" and "Hey Siri, call Karen." Chapter 3, "Using Siri," covers how to interact with Siri on your Watch in more depth.

If you don't speak right away, tap the microphone icon to speak.

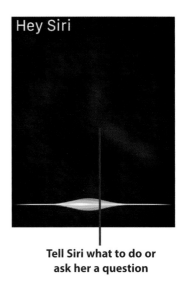

Tell Siri what to do or ask her a question

Tap to speak

Updating Your Apple Watch

From time to time, Apple will release an update for your Apple Watch. Updates can fix bugs and add new features. When a new update is available, you will see a red badge on the corner of the Watch app on your iPhone. Tap on the Watch app, and then tap General and choose Software Update. Tap Download and Install to download the Watch update, prepare it, and install it on your Watch. Your Watch must be on its charger, and have more than 50% charge before you can complete the update. Once the update is ready, the Watch app on your iPhone sends it to your Watch. On your Watch screen, you see a notice telling you that the update will start in 30 seconds. You will be able to tap Not Now to delay the update, or tap Install to install it immediately. See Chapter 8, "Installing and Managing Watch Apps," for more information on this topic.

Tap to update your Watch

Customize your
watch face

In this chapter, you learn how to customize your Apple Watch to suit your needs. Topics include the following:

→ Choosing and customizing your watch faces
→ Rearranging your app icons
→ Managing Glances

Personalizing Your Apple Watch

Your Watch already looks beautiful, but you can make it your own by personalizing the way it looks and functions to suit your personality and the way you want your Apple Watch to work for you.

Choosing and Customizing Your Watch Face

Your Apple Watch comes pre-installed with a number of watch faces. You can choose a different watch face to suit your mood, customize the watch face, and even create new watch faces.

Choose a New Watch Face

Your Watch comes with 13 watch faces preloaded. Here is how to choose one.

1. Force Touch on the current watch face.

2. Swipe left and right to see all the available watch faces.

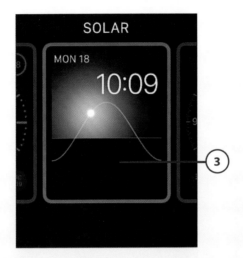

3. Tap a watch face to use it.

Customize an Existing Watch Face

Most watch faces can be customized by adding, removing, or changing the complications that are visible. In some cases, you can also change watch face colors and the detail
shown on the face. You can use the following steps to customize the watch face you are
currently using, or customize a different watch face before you start using it.

1. Force Touch on the current watch face.

2. To keep your current watch face, skip this step and move on to step 3 to begin customizing. To change to another watch face, swipe left and right to see all the available watch faces.

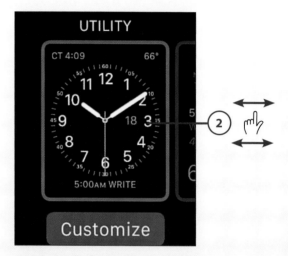

3. Tap Customize. If you do not see the word Customize under the watch face, that particular watch face cannot be customized.

4. Turn the Digital Crown to choose the amount of numeric detail shown on the watch face. Some watch faces do not allow changing the numeric detail.

5. Swipe from right to left to move to the next customization screen.

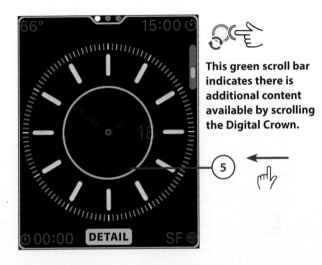

This green scroll bar indicates there is additional content available by scrolling the Digital Crown.

6. Turn the Digital Crown to choose the color of the second hand. On some watch faces, the color customization screen allows you to choose the color of the watch face itself.

7. Swipe from right to left to move to the next customization screen.

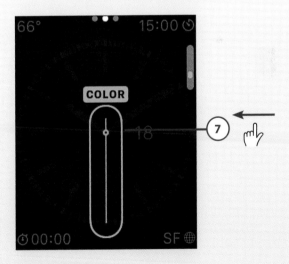

What Are Complications?

Makers of mechanical watches use the term "complications" to describe any mechanical watch function that is in addition to displaying the time in hours and minutes. In fact, a watch that only shows the hours and minutes is said to have a simple movement. Because mechanical watches are made using tiny gears, springs, and other mechanical pieces, adding extra functionality is complicated, and hence adding something such as the date to the display is said to be a complication. This is true not only in watch construction, but when the watch needs to be repaired. Some examples of mechanical watch complications include a chronograph, moon phases, and displaying time in different times zones. When Apple designed the Apple Watch, they wanted to keep the traditional language surrounding watches, and so a watch face on your Apple Watch can include complications, which are essentially icons that show additional information such as the time in a different time zone or the weather. Watch apps that you install might include additional complications.

8. Tap the date complication and turn the Digital Crown to scroll between Off and Date. Off means that the complication is not shown, and Date means the face displays the day of the month.

9. Tap the complication in the top-right of the screen.

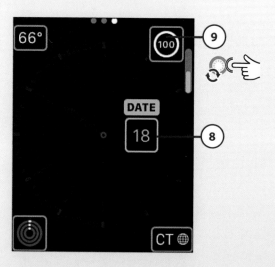

10. Turn the Digital Crown to scroll through all of the available complications to choose one for this position on the watch face. If you choose Off, no complication is shown at this position.

11. Tap the three remaining complication positions and turn the Digital Crown to choose a complication for each position, or choose Off to show no complication at that position.

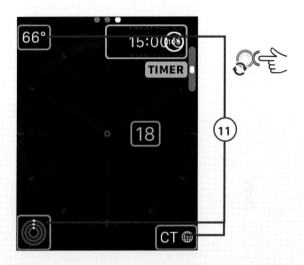

12. Press the Digital Crown or Force Touch after you have finished making all the customizations to the watch face. You can also just wait for 5–10 seconds and your changes will be saved.

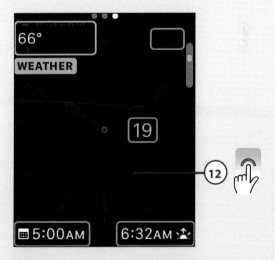

13. Tap the now customized watch face to start using it.

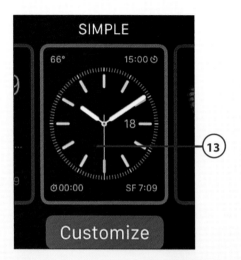

Create a New Version of an Existing Watch Face

You can create new versions of existing watch faces so that you can switch between them quickly in the future. This would be useful if you want to use the same type of watch face, but customized for different situations.

1. Force Touch on the current watch face.

2. Swipe from right to left until you see the plus (+) symbol.

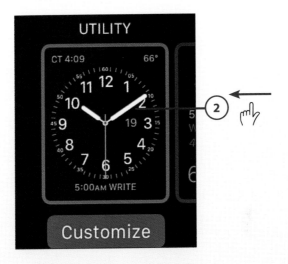

3. Tap the plus symbol.

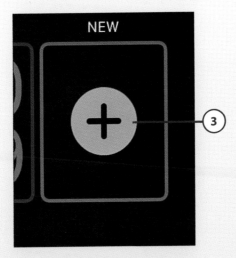

4. Turn the Digital Crown to choose the watch face for which you want to make a new version.

5. Tap the watch face to select it.

6. Follow the steps in the previous section, "Customize an Existing Watch Face," to customize your new watch face.

Delete a Watch Face

You can delete any watch face, including the ones that came pre-installed and any versions you may have created.

1. Force Touch on the current watch face.

2. Swipe left and right to find the watch face you want to delete.

3. Swipe the watch face up.

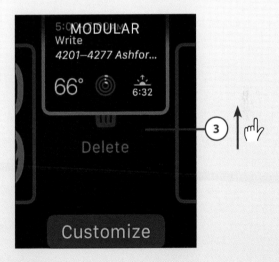

4. Tap Delete.

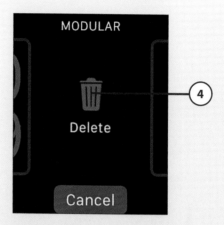

What If I Delete One of the Pre-installed Watch Faces?

If you accidentally delete one of the pre-installed watch faces, you can create a new version of it by following the steps in the section "Create a New Version of an Existing Watch Face."

Using the Photo Album and Photo Watch Faces

New! The Photo Album watch face uses the photo album you have chosen to synchronize to your Watch. Each time you lift your wrist to see the time, a new randomly selected photo from that photo album is displayed along with the time. The Photo watch face shows one photo from the synchronized photo album. Here is how to use the Photo and Photo Album watch faces.

Synchronize a Photo Album

Before you use the Photo or Photo Album watch faces, you must first synchronize a photo album from the Photos application on your Mac to your Watch. You may choose to create a new album just for this purpose or use an existing one.

1. Tap the Watch app on your iPhone.

2. Swipe up until you see Photos. Tap Photos.

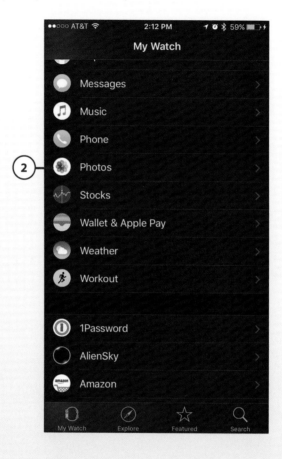

3. Tap Synced Album.

4. Tap the name of the album you want to synchronize to your Watch. In this example, the Favorites album is chosen.

5. Tap Photos to return to the previous screen.

6. Tap Photos Limit.

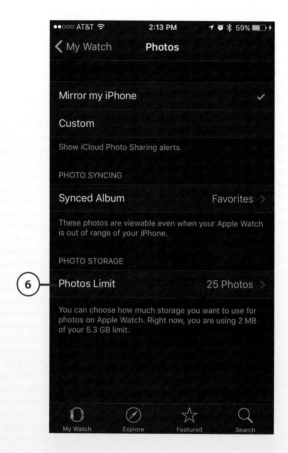

7. Choose the maximum number of photos you want to synchronize from the chosen photo album to your Watch. This limits the number of photos that synchronize to your Watch, even if there are more photos in the photo album.

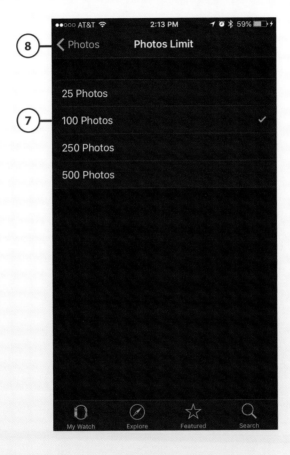

8. Tap Photos to return to the previous screen.

Choose The Photo Album Watch Face

Now that you have a photo album synchronized to your Watch, you can choose the Photo Album watch face.

1. Force Touch the watch face.

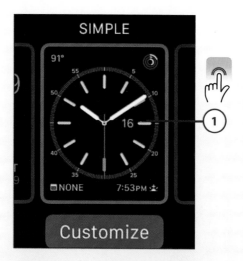

2. Swipe left or right until you find the Photo Album watch face.

3. Tap the Photo Album watch face to choose it.

Create a Photo Watch Face

Now that you have a photo album synchronized to your Watch, you can create one or more Photo watch faces, each with their own photo. You can repeat these steps as many times as you like to create many Photo watch faces each with their own photo.

1. Press the Digital Crown to see a list of your Watch apps.

2. Tap the Photos Watch app.

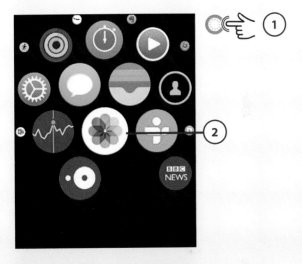

3. Force Touch a photo that you want to use as a new Photo watch face.

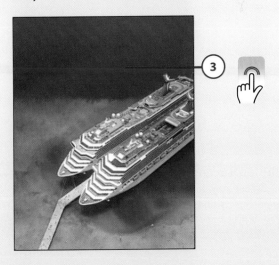

4. Tap Create Watch Face.

5. A new watch face is created using the photo as its background.

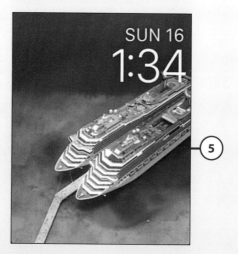

Time Lapse Watch Face

The Time Lapse watch face plays a time lapse of cities and landmarks around the world, according to the time of day. For example, if it is morning when you lift your wrist to see the time, a time lapse of the city or landmark you have chosen plays for the morning hours. You can customize the Time Lapse watch face and choose different cities and landmarks including Mack Lake, New York, Hong Kong, London, Paris, and Shanghai.

Change Overall Watch Face Functionality

From your iPhone, you can control overall watch face settings, including whether you want to show 24-hour time, show the Notifications Indicator, and even change the monogram letters used.

1. On your iPhone, tap the Apple Watch app icon.

2. Scroll down until you see the Clock icon and then tap it.

3. Tap to enable or disable displaying the time in 24-hour format when you are using a digital watch face. Analog watch faces do not show a 24-hour clock.

4. Tap to choose whether you want your Watch to receive Timer and Alarm alerts from your iPhone. When this is turned on, you are able to choose to snooze or dismiss an alarm playing on your iPhone.

5. Tap to choose whether you want a red dot to appear at the top of the Watch screen to indicate that you have unread notifications.

6. Tap to change the monogram that is used by the Color watch face. It defaults to the first letters of your first and last names, but you can change that.

7. Tap to change the default acronyms used by your Watch to symbolize cities you have chosen to see in the World Clock complication. This is useful if you are using the World Clock complication and are confused by the letters that are being used.

8. Tap My Watch to save your changes and return to the previous screen.

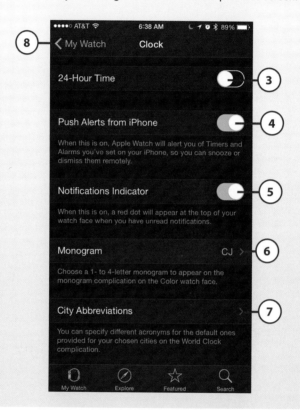

>>>Go Further

MAKE YOUR WATCH DISPLAY TIME AHEAD OF THE ACTUAL TIME

You may have always set your clocks and watches to show time a few minutes ahead of the actual time so that you are tricked into getting to meetings and other appointments on time. You can do this with your Apple Watch too. Press the Digital Crown to show the apps. Tap the Settings app (the gear icon) and then tap Time. Tap the gray bar displaying the time. Use the Digital Crown to choose how many minutes ahead of real time your Watch should display. Tap Set to save your change. Although your Apple Watch now shows time ahead of the actual time, any alarms you have set still trigger at the correct time and any notifications for meetings still appear at the correct time.

Set how many minutes ahead your Watch should display

Time Travel with Your Watch

Time Traveling with your Watch allows you to look ahead into the future, or look back at the past to see what will be happening in the future, or be reminded of what has already happened. While looking at any watch face (with the exception of Time Lapse, Photo Album, and Photo watch faces), turn the Digital Crown to time travel forward and backward through time. Your watch face shows the date, time, and information that occurred at that time in the past, or that will occur at that time in the future. For example, if you time travel forward in time, you see appointments appear, and even complications, showing things like temperature, and sunrise/sunset that appear as they will be in the future. Press the Digital Crown to return to real time.

Complications accurate during Time Travel

Rearranging App Icons and Activating Airplane Mode

The more apps you install on your Watch, the more app icons you see on your Home Screen (list of apps). You might want to rearrange the app icons to make the ones you routinely use easier to access. You can also coordinate Airplane Mode between your iPhone and Apple Watch.

Move App Icons

You might want to move the icons for the apps you use more often closer to the center of the app list. Here is how.

1. On your iPhone, tap the Apple Watch app icon.

2. Tap App Layout.

3. Touch and hold on the app icon that you want to move. The icon gets a bit larger, indicating it can be moved. In this example, we are going to move the Evernote app icon.

4. Drag the app icon to its new position. As you drag it, other app icons move out of its way. When you have the app icon in the desired position, lift your finger to release it.

5. Tap My Watch to save your changes and return to the previous screen.

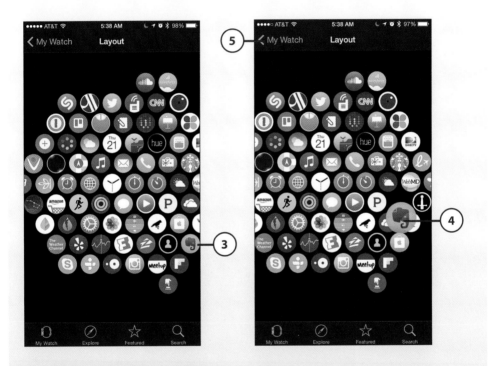

Configure Do Not Disturb

When enabled, Do Not Disturb silences all alerts and notifications on your Apple Watch. By default, Do Not Disturb on your Watch mirrors how it is set up on your iPhone. You can choose to control Do Not Disturb on your Watch separately.

1. On your iPhone, tap the Apple Watch app icon.

2. Tap General.

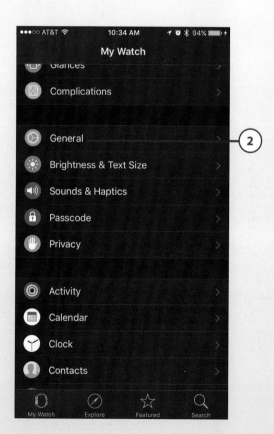

3. Tap Do Not Disturb.

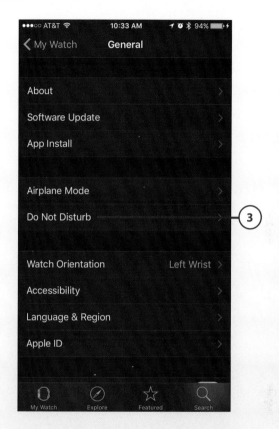

4. Tap the On/Off slider to choose whether you want Do Not Disturb mode to be mirrored between your iPhone and Apple Watch.

What Is the Best Way to Configure Do Not Disturb?

By default, your Apple Watch mirrors your iPhone for Do Not Disturb mode. This means that when Do Not Disturb is enabled or disabled on your iPhone (manually or automatically), your Watch also enables or disables Do Not Disturb to mirror your iPhone. It also means that if you manually enable Do Not Disturb on your Apple Watch, your iPhone mirrors that setting. If you turn off the Do Not Disturb Mirror iPhone setting, it simply means that your Watch and iPhone no longer mirror each other for Do Not Disturb, but that doesn't mean your iPhone does not automatically enable Do Not Disturb if you have set it up to. That still happens as it always has. While your iPhone has Do Not Disturb enabled, because your

Watch receives all of its alerts from your iPhone, your Watch only receives alerts from local apps running on your Watch, such as the Activity app. Because you can set up an automatic Do Not Disturb period on your iPhone, it is best to leave the Do Not Disturb Mirror iPhone setting set to On so that you are not disturbed by any alerts during the Do Not Disturb period. To configure automatic Do Not Disturb (for example, during hours you are asleep), on your iPhone tap Settings, tap Do Not Disturb, tap Scheduled, and then set up the automatic Do Not Disturb how you like it.

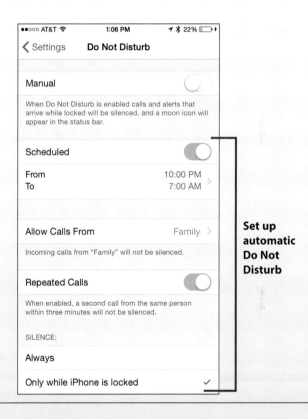

Manually Enable or Disable Do Not Disturb on Your Watch

The quickest way to enable or disable Do Not Disturb on your Watch is to use the Settings Glance. To do this, swipe up from the bottom of your Watch screen. If you do not see the Settings Glance, swipe from left to right until you see it. Tap the Do Not Disturb icon (the moon). The other way is to open the Settings app and tap Do Not Disturb. See "Managing Glances" for more on working with Glances on your Watch.

Coordinate Airplane Mode

Some airlines still insist on having you put your electronic devices into Airplane Mode. You can make this slightly less painful by having your iPhone and Apple Watch coordinate Airplane Mode so you only have to enable it on one device and the other mirrors this setting.

1. On your iPhone, tap the Apple Watch app icon.

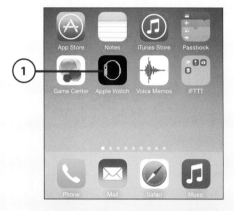

2. Tap General.

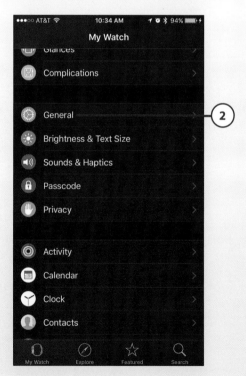

3. Tap Airplane Mode.

4. Tap the On/Off slider to the On position to enable mirroring the iPhone's Airplane Mode setting. When this setting is On, if you enable Airplane Mode on your iPhone, your Apple Watch also changes its Airplane Mode setting, and if you make the change on your Apple Watch, your iPhone changes its setting to match.

5. Tap General to return to the previous screen.

THE REALITY OF AIRPLANE MODE MIRRORING

If you do turn on Airplane Mode mirroring between your iPhone and your Watch, bear in mind that you are still bound by the laws of physics. If you turn Airplane Mode on, what actually happens is that all the radios on your iPhone and Watch turn off. So, at that point, your iPhone and Watch have no way of communicating with each other. If you then turn Airplane Mode off on your iPhone, your Watch still has all its radios turned off and there is no way to get a signal to your Watch to tell it to turn Airplane Mode off. The same is true if you turn off Airplane Mode on your Watch; your iPhone still has its radios off and there is no way to communicate with it. So just remember that if you mirror Airplane Mode, it will work great for turning on Airplane Mode, but you still need to turn off Airplane Mode manually on both your iPhone and Watch.

Managing Glances

Glances are similar to Widgets on your iPhone. They provide real-time information and extend controls from apps. Glances are added or removed based on the apps you have installed on your Watch. You can rearrange the order in which Glances appear as well as choose which Glances you want to see and which ones to hide.

Swipe Up for Glances

While any watch face is visible, swipe up from the bottom of your Watch screen to see and interact with Glances. Swipe left and right to scroll through all available Glances.

Rearranging Glances

With the exception of the Settings Glance, which is always the first in the series of Glances, you can rearrange the order in which Glances appear.

1. On your iPhone, tap the Apple Watch app icon.

2. Tap Glances.

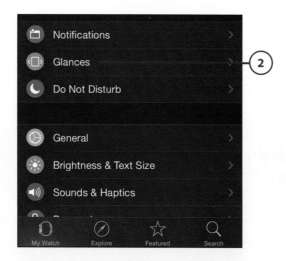

3. Tap Edit.

4. Use the Glance anchor and move it up and down the list of Glances to reposition it. The higher up the list you move the Glance, the further to the left it appears on your Watch. The lower on the list you move the Glance, the further to the right it appears on your Watch.

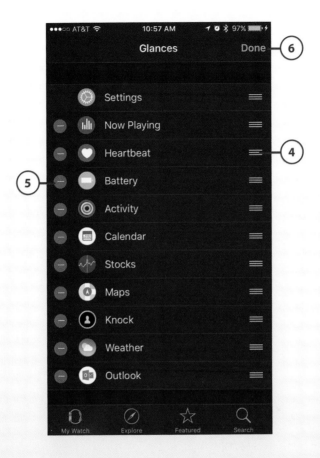

5. Tap to hide (or not include) a Glance. Once hidden (or not included), it does not appear on your Watch, but it is still available to use in the future, if you return to this setting list and re-enable it.

6. Tap Done to save your changes.

Add Glances

You may have Glances that were installed with one of the Watch apps you installed, but are not being included in the Glances list. To add them to the Glances list, or to add back one you previously removed from the list, follow these steps.

1. On your iPhone, tap the Apple Watch app icon.

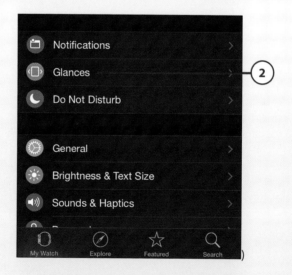

2. Tap Glances.

3. Tap Edit.

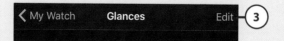

4. Scroll down until you see the Glances in the Do Not Include list.

5. Tap the green circle to add a Glance to the list of Glances available on your Watch.

6. Tap Done to save your changes.

Configuring General Watch Settings

In General Settings, you are able to change a variety of settings, including renaming your Apple Watch, configuring accessibility, and enabling or disabling Handoff, among other things.

Change General Settings

In the General Settings screen, you can change some settings, you can also view information such as how much memory each app is using. You can even reset your Watch back to factory settings.

1. On your iPhone, tap the Apple Watch app icon.

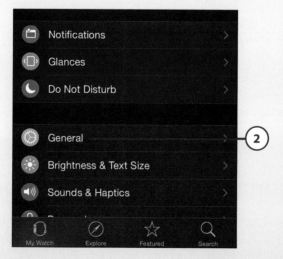

2. Tap General.

3. Tap About to see information about your Watch, including the number of photos and apps installed on your Watch and Watch OS version information. You can also rename your Apple Watch.

4. Tap Software Update to manually check to see if there is a Watch OS update for your Watch.

5. Tap App Install to choose whether you want Watch apps automatically downloaded and installed on your Watch, if an app on your iPhone includes a Watch app. If you turn this off, you need to manually choose the Watch apps you want to install.

6. Tap Watch Orientation to choose on which wrist you wear your Watch and whether you want the Digital Crown on the left or right side.

7. Tap Accessibility to access a number of accessibility settings that can help you use your Watch. (See the next task, "Add Accessibility," for more information on these settings.)

8. Tap Language & Region to choose the language used on your Watch, the region format, and the type of calendar your Watch uses.

9. Tap Apple ID to view the Apple ID that is being used on your Watch.

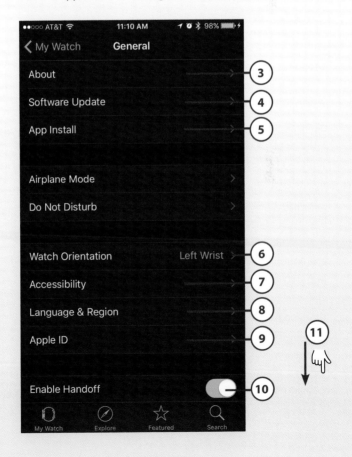

10.   Tap the On/Off switch to enable or disable Handoff.

What Is Handoff?

When Handoff is turned on, your iPhone and your Mac (if you are near your Mac) are able to pick up where you left off, if you decide to continue working on the same app on your iPhone or Mac that you were previously using on your Watch. Your iPhone displays the app's icon on the bottom left of the lock screen. Swiping that icon up allows you to continue where you left off on your Watch.

11.   Scroll down for more settings.

12.   Tap the On/Off switch to enable or disable Wrist Detection.

What Is Wrist Detection?

When Wrist Detection is turned on, your Watch can detect your skin, which allows it to determine whether it is on your wrist. When you take your Watch off, and you have set a lock code, your Watch detects that it is no longer in contact with your skin, and it locks. When you put your Watch back on, your Watch detects this and displays the passcode screen. Wrist Detection also determines when you raise your wrist. When it detects that you have raised your wrist, it shows you the time, the last Watch app you were using, or the latest notification.

13.   Tap Wake Screen to choose whether you want your Watch to wake up when you raise your wrist. You can also choose what you see when you raise your wrist. You can choose to always see the time or to see the last app you were using.

14.   Tap the On/Off switch to enable or disable Nightstand Mode. When enabled, the time will be displayed horizontally while your Watch is charging, and the screen will slowly brighten as it gets close to your morning alarm.

15.   Tap Usage to see a list of all apps and how much memory they are using, how much time you have used your Watch, how much time is left on the battery, and how much time your Watch lasts, if it enters Power Reserve Mode.

16.   Tap Reset to see the reset options. You can reset all content and settings on your Watch and return it to how it came out of the box, reset only the Home Screen (app icon) layout, or reset only the contacts and calendar data from your Watch.

17.   Tap My Watch to save your changes and return to the previous screen.

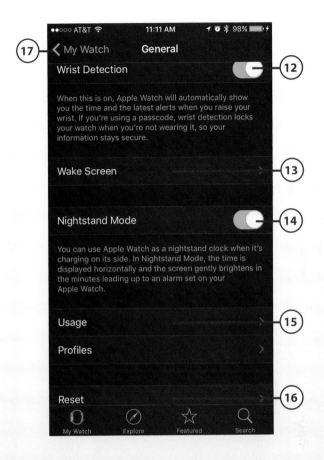

Add Accessibility

If you have vision or hearing limitations, Accessibility allows you to makes changes to the way your Watch behaves, and how you interact with it. Do steps 1, 2, and 7 in the previous section to reach the Accessibility screen before continuing with these steps.

1. Tap to enable VoiceOver and customize the way it works. VoiceOver can speak the time, onscreen text, and all actions you take. You can control the rate and volume at which the words are spoken, and you can set VoiceOver to speak the time when you raise your wrist.

2. Tap to enable Zoom. When this option is enabled, you can double-tap with two fingers on your Watch screen to activate a magnifying window. Using two fingers, you can drag the magnifier window around the screen.

3. Tap to enable Grayscale. When this option is enabled, your Watch screen stops using colors and everything appears in grayscale.

4. Tap to enable Bold Text. Choosing this option requires your Watch to restart.

5. Tap to enable Reduce Motion. When this option is enabled, animations are limited, as is zooming in to an app from the Home Screen using the Digital Crown.

6. Tap to enable Reduce Transparency. When this option is enabled, contrast on certain backgrounds is improved to make the screens easier to read.

7. Tap to enable On/Off Labels. When this option is enabled, a 1 or 0 will appear in an On/Off switch, indicating that it is on or off.

8. Scroll down for more settings.

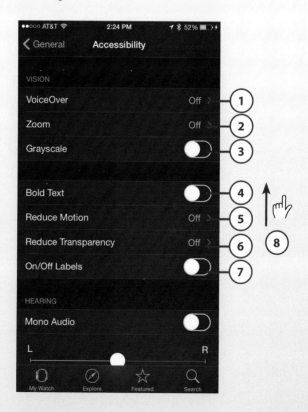

9. Tap the Mono Audio switch to choose whether you only want to hear audio in mono when playing back stereo audio. This is useful if you have paired a stereo Bluetooth headset with your Watch.

10. Drag the slider to control whether audio is more prominent on the left or right ear when you're playing stereo audio.

11. Tap to choose whether you want to be able to triple-press the Digital Crown to enable or disable VoiceOver or Zoom accessibility functions.

12. Tap General to save your changes and return to the previous screen.

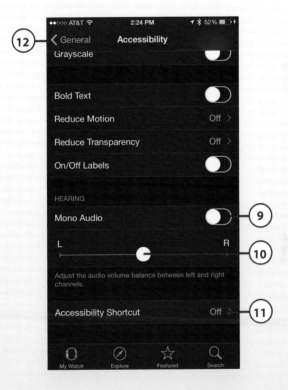

Changing General Settings on Your Watch

You can change some of the General settings on your Apple Watch. To do this, press the Digital Crown to see the Home Screen. Tap the Settings icon (the gear) and then tap General. You can change the Orientation, Active on Wrist Raise, and Accessibility settings. You can also enable or disable the ability to raise your wrist and say "Hey Siri" to activate Siri.

Changing Screen, Sound, and Haptics Settings

You can change the screen brightness, text size, and whether the text is bold or regular, plus control the alert volume and adjust the strength of the haptic feedback.

Adjust Brightness and Text Size

You can adjust your Watch screen brightness, the size of the text, and decide if you want all text to be shown in bold.

1. On your iPhone, tap the Apple Watch app icon.

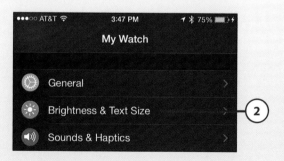

2. Tap Brightness & Text Size.

3. Drag the slider to control the brightness of your Watch screen.

4. Drag the slider to control the size of the text displayed on your Watch.

5. Tap to enable Bold Text. When this option is enabled, text displayed on your Watch is bold. Choosing this option requires your Watch to restart.

6. Tap My Watch to save your changes and return to the previous screen.

Changing Brightness and Text Size Settings on Your Watch

You can change the same Brightness and Text Size settings right on your Watch. To do this, tap the Settings icon (the gear) and then tap Brightness & Text Size.

Adjust Sounds and Haptics

You can adjust the volume of alert sounds on your Watch, control the strength of the haptic feedback (the tap on your wrist), and choose whether to mute your Watch when you cover the screen.

1. On your iPhone, tap the Apple Watch app icon.

2. Tap Sounds & Haptics.

3. Drag the slider to control the volume of the sound that plays when you receive an alert on your Watch.

4. Tap the On/Off switch to enable or disable Silent Mode. When Silent Mode is enabled, alert sounds are muted.

5. Drag the slider to control the strength of the haptic feedback (the tap on your wrist). If you cannot feel the tap, or don't feel that it is noticeable enough, increase the strength here.

6. Tap the On/Off switch to enable or disable receiving a prominent tap on your wrist ahead of common alerts. If you feel that you are missing alerts on your Watch, turn this on.

7. Tap the On/Off switch to enable or disable the ability to mute your Watch when you place your hand over the Watch screen for three seconds.

8. Tap My Watch to save your changes and return to the previous screen.

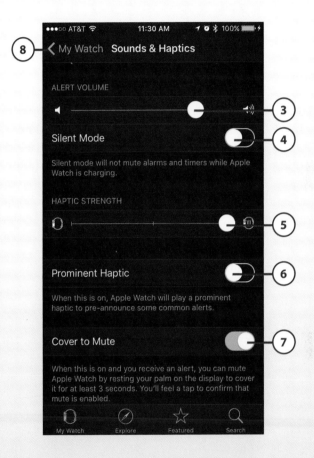

Changing Sounds & Haptics Settings on Your Watch

You can change the same Sounds & Haptics settings (with the exception of Cover to Mute) right on your Watch. To do this, tap the Settings icon (the gear) and then tap Sounds & Haptics.

Control Notifications

In the Apple Watch app, you can create a select list of third-party apps that have permission to send notifications to you on your Apple Watch as well as change the way that the built-in Watch apps notify you.

1. On your iPhone, tap the Apple Watch app icon.

2. Tap Notifications.

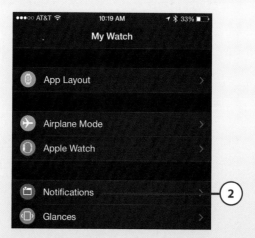

3. Tap the On/Off slider to choose whether you want to see the red dot on your Watch, indicating that you have unread notifications. If you turn this off, the red dot does not appear for unread notifications; however, you still receive all notifications.

4. Tap the On/Off slider to choose whether you want to see the contents of a notification when you lift your wrist. If this is turned on, when you lift your wrist to view a notification, all you see is the icon from the app that sent the notification and, sometimes, who the notification is from. Only after you tap on the notification are you able to see it in full.

Why Would You Use Notification Privacy?

When you feel a tap on your wrist to indicate a new notification has arrived, you can lift your wrist to view it. Someone sitting behind you may also be able to see the notification as it appears on your Watch. In some situations, you might want to keep your notifications private, so if you enable Notification Privacy, you can choose to first move to a more private area and then tap on the notification to see it in full.

5. Scroll down to change how built-in apps notify you. See the "Changing Settings for Built-in Watch Apps" section, later in this chapter, for specifics on setting notifications for each of these apps.

Changing Passcode-Related Settings

You can enable or disable a passcode on your Watch, choose to use your iPhone to enter your Watch passcode, and even set your Watch to wipe itself if the passcode is entered incorrectly 10 times.

1. Tap the Apple Watch app icon.

2. Tap Passcode.

3. Tap to turn the passcode off. When you turn your passcode off, you will need to enter the current passcode to continue.

4. Tap to change your Watch passcode. When you change your passcode, you need to enter the current passcode to continue.

5. Tap the On/Off switch to enable or disable a simple four-digit Watch passcode. If you turn this off, you are required to use your iPhone to enter a longer passcode to unlock your Watch.

6. Tap the On/Off switch to enable or disable the ability to unlock your Watch when you unlock your iPhone. With this turned on, your Watch unlocks when you unlock your iPhone and you do not need to enter the passcode on your Watch.

7. Tap the On/Off switch to enable or disable the ability for your Watch to wipe itself, if someone tries to enter your passcode incorrectly 10 times.

8. Tap My Watch to save your changes and return to the previous screen.

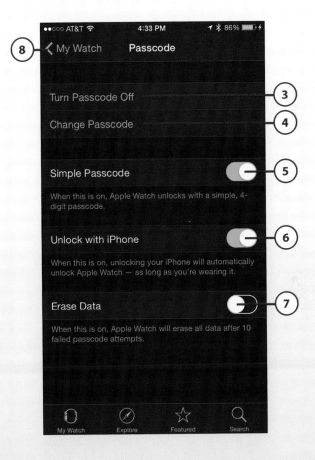

Changing Passcode Settings on Your Watch

You can change the same Passcode settings right on your Watch. To do this, tap the Settings icon (the gear) and then tap Passcode.

Configuring Motion and Fitness Privacy Settings

You can choose to allow your Watch to gather your heart rate and movement so it can calculate how many calories you are burning and your fitness level.

1. On your iPhone, tap the Apple Watch app icon.

2. Tap Privacy.

3. Tap Motion & Fitness.

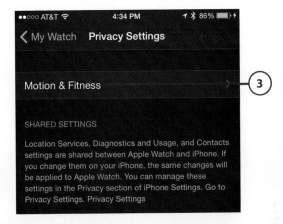

4. Tap the On/Off switch to choose whether you want to allow your Watch to sample your heart rate at regular intervals. If you turn this off, your Watch is no longer able to calculate calories burned.

5. Tap the On/Off switch to choose whether you want to allow your Watch to track your body movement. If you turn this off, your Watch can no longer determine if you are moving and how much.

6. Tap Privacy Settings to save your changes and return to the previous screen.

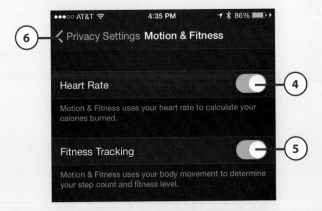

Change Your Personal Information

The Activity app on your Watch and iPhone keeps track of your calories burned and fitness level by sampling your heart rate and tracking body movement; however, it is not accurate unless you have entered in your personal information correctly. If you need to correct your birthdate, sex, height, or weight, open the Apple Watch app on your iPhone, tap the Health icon, and then tap Edit to make the changes.

Changing Settings for Built-in Watch Apps

You can adjust the settings for the built-in Watch apps, including Activity, Calendar, Clock, Contacts, Friends, Mail, Maps, and more.

1. On your iPhone, tap the Apple Watch app icon, scroll down and tap each of the built-in apps, and follow the steps in the sections that follow to change settings for each of the built-in Watch apps.

Activity

You can adjust whether the Activity app appears in the Glances view, what information it shows, and how often it is shown.

1. Tap the On/Off switch to choose whether you want Activity to appear in the list of Glances.

2. Tap the On/Off switch to choose whether you want to mute the activity reminders and alerts for one day.

3. Tap the On/Off switch to choose whether you want the Activity app to remind you to stand up during the day.

4. Tap Progress Updates to choose whether you want the Activity app to provide you with progress updates, and if so, how often.

5. Tap the Goal Completions On/Off switch to choose whether you want the Activity app to notify you when you reach your daily move goals.

6. Scroll down for more options.

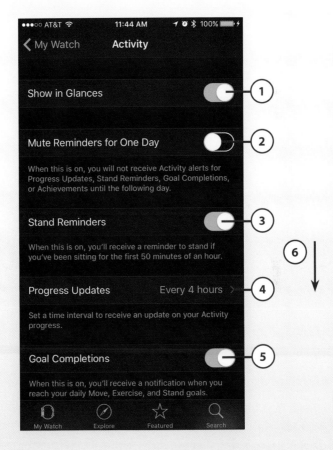

7. Tap the Achievements On/Off switch to choose whether you want the Activity app to notify you when you reach a movement milestone.

8. Tap the Weekly Summary On/Off switch to choose whether you want the Activity app to provide you with your weekly summary on the first day of a new week.

9. Tap My Watch to save your changes and return to the previous screen.

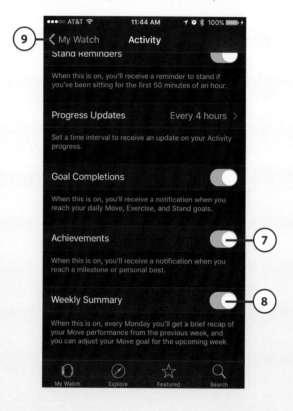

Calendar

You can adjust whether the Calendar app appears in the Glances view, and decide if you want the Calendar alerts to mirror the Calendar app on your iPhone, or you can choose specific alerts just for your Watch.

1. Tap the Mirror my iPhone option to have the alerts for the Calendar app on your Watch to mirror how you have them set up on your iPhone, or tap Custom to choose how you want Calendar on your Watch to alert you. If you chose Mirror my iPhone, skip to step 7.

2. Tap the Show Alerts On/Off switch to choose whether you want the Calendar app on your Watch app to show alerts. (If you previously chose to turn all alerts off for your Watch, or for the Calendar app itself, skip to step 7.)

3. Tap Upcoming Events to choose whether you want to receive upcoming and event alerts on your Watch, and if you do, whether you want to be notified by sound, haptic feedback, or both.

4. Tap Invitations to choose whether you want to receive event invitation alerts on your Watch, and if you do, whether you want to be notified by sound, haptic feedback, or both.

5. Tap Invitee Responses to choose whether you want to receive alerts for responses from people you invite to meetings on your Watch, and if you do, whether you want to be notified by sound, haptic feedback, or both.

6. Tap Shared Calendar Alerts to choose whether you want to receive shared calendar alerts on your Watch, and if you do, whether you want to be notified by sound, haptic feedback, or both.

7. Tap My Watch to save your changes and return to the previous screen.

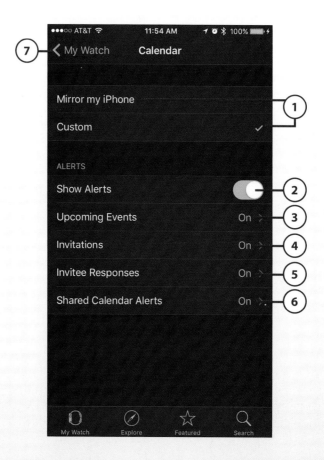

Clock

You can adjust how the Clock app works on your Watch, including choosing 24-hour time and your monogram.

1. Tap the 24-Hour Time On/Off switch to choose whether you want your Watch to show time in a 24-hour format any time a digital clock is shown. When the setting is Off, it shows a 12-hour format. This setting affects complications that show time in a digital format as well as any watch faces that show time in a digital format. Analog watch faces continue to show time in a 12-hour format.

2. Tap the Push Alerts from iPhone On/Off switch to choose whether you want to receive push alerts from apps running on your iPhone. If you turn this off, you stop receiving all alerts and notifications from your iPhone with the exception of timers and alarms, but continue to receive alerts and notifications from apps running on your Watch.

3. Tap the Notifications Indicator On/Off switch to choose whether you want the red dot to appear on your watch face when you have unread alerts or notifications. If you turn this off, alerts and notifications still come to your Watch, you just won't see an indication that you have unread alerts. With this off, you have to swipe down from the top of the screen periodically to check for missed alerts.

4. Tap Monogram to change the monogram that appears when you use the monogram complication for the Color watch face. The first letters from your first and last names are used automatically. You can change the monogram used and choose a new monogram of up to four letters.

5. Tap City Abbreviations to change the acronyms that have been automatically chosen for cities in the World Clock complication. For example, the automatically chosen acronym for Cape Town is CT, but you may want to see it as CPT.

6. Tap My Watch to save your changes and return to the previous screen.

Contacts

In this group of settings, you can decide if you want the contact information displayed on your Watch to mirror how you have it configured to display in the Contacts app on your iPhone, or you can choose a specific configuration for your Watch.

1. Tap Mirror my iPhone to have the contact information displayed on your Watch to mirror how you have contact information set up to display on your iPhone. If you chose Mirror my iPhone, skip to step 5. Otherwise, tap Custom and continue with step 2.

2. Tap Sort Order to change the way in which contacts are sorted. You can choose to sort by Last, First or First, Last.

3. Tap Display Order to change the way in which contacts are displayed. You can choose to display names as Last, First or First, Last.

4. Tap Short Name to choose how a contact's short name is derived. You can choose to use short names and decide how the short name is formatted. Your choices include first name and last initial, first initial and last name, first name only, and last name only. You can also choose to use a contact's nickname (if they have one).

5. Tap My Watch to save your changes and return to the previous screen.

Friends

The Friends app controls which contacts you see when you press the Side Button on your Watch. Choose the contacts to add to the Friends app, what position they are in the Friends Selector, and add or remove friends from the Friends app. You can have one or more groups of 12 friends per group.

1. Tap Group Name to name the group of friends on this screen.

2. Tap an existing friend's initials to select that friend.

3. Tap the delete icon to delete the selected friend from the current group.

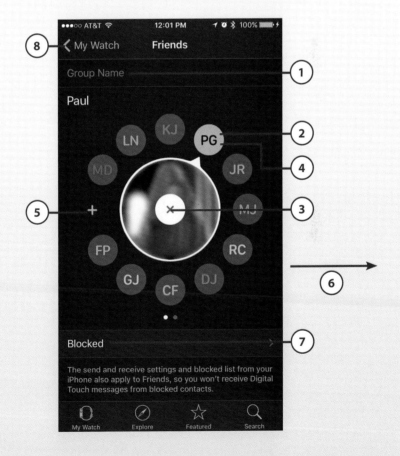

4. Touch and hold a friend to reposition them in the group.

5. Tap the add icon to add a new frind to the group.

6. Swipe left to see the next group of friends. While viewing the new group, use steps 1 – 5 to edit the group.

7. Tap Blocked to choose contacts you want to block from communicating with you.

8. Tap My Watch to save your changes and return to the previous screen.

Mail

These settings enable you to decide if you want your mail shown, and the way you are alerted for mail information, on your Watch to mirror how you have it configured in the Mail app on your iPhone, or choose a custom configuration for your Watch.

1. Tap Mirror my iPhone to have the mail display configuration and alerts on your Watch mirror how you have them set up on your iPhone, or you can tap Custom to choose settings specific to your Watch. If you chose Mirror my iPhone, skip to step 9.

2. Tap Show Alerts to choose whether you want to show alerts for new emails. If you turn this off, skip to step 4.

3. Tap each mail account and choose whether you want to be notified for new emails arriving into the mail account, and if you want to be notified by sound, haptic feedback (tap), or both.

4. Tap Include Mail to choose which mail accounts you want to include mail from on your Watch.

5. Tap Message Preview to choose whether you want to see a preview of an email in the alert, and whether you want to see just the first line or the first two lines of the email.

6. Tap Default Replies to view and edit the list of default replies you can use when replying to an email.

7. Tap Signature to view or edit the signature that appears in the footer of all emails you compose or reply to from your Watch.

8. Tap Flag Style to choose whether you want to see a colored dot or a flag when you choose to flag an email on your Watch.

9. Tap Ask Before Deleting to decide if you want to be asked before an email is deleted.

10. Tap Organize By Thread to choose whether you want to have emails organized by email thread when emails are displayed on your Watch.

11. Tap My Watch to save your changes and return to the previous screen.

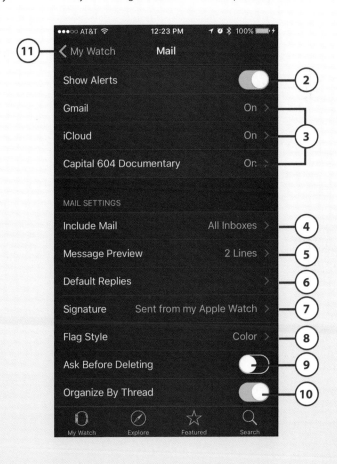

Maps

Use these settings to decide if you want Maps to appear in the Glances list, and choose if you want to be alerted during turn-by-turn navigation.

1. Tap Show in Glances to choose whether you want the Maps Watch app to appear in the Glances list.

2. Tap Turn Alerts to choose whether you want to be alerted at each turn when using turn-by-turn navigation.

3. Tap My Watch to save your changes and return to the previous screen.

Messages

Use the Messages settings to decide if you want the way in which messages (iMessage and SMS) are shown, and the way you are alerted for messages on your Watch, to mirror how you have it configured on your iPhone, or you can choose a custom configuration for your Watch.

1. Tap Mirror my iPhone to have the Messages display configuration and alerts on your Watch mirror how you have them set up on your iPhone. Alternatively, tap Custom to choose settings specific to your Watch. If you chose Mirror my iPhone, skip to step 6.

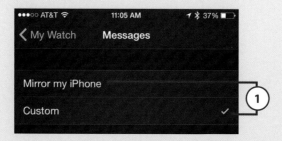

2. Tap Show Alerts to choose whether you want to show alerts for new messages. If you turn this off, skip to step 7.

3. Tap Sound to choose whether you want to hear a sound when new messages arrive.

4. Tap Haptic to choose whether you want to feel a tap on your wrist when new messages arrive.

5. Tap Repeat Alerts to choose if your Watch should repeat an alert for a new message if you ignore it, and if so, how many times the alert is repeated. You can choose between 1 and 10 repeat notifications.

6. Tap Audio Messages to decide how you want dictated replies to messages to be sent. You can choose to always send the audio of your dictation or just the dictated text, or you can opt to choose each time.

7. Tap Default Replies to edit the default replies that you can send as replies to messages.

8. Tap Send Read Receipts to choose whether you want to send read receipts for messages you have read on your Watch.

9. Tap My Watch to save your changes and return to the previous screen.

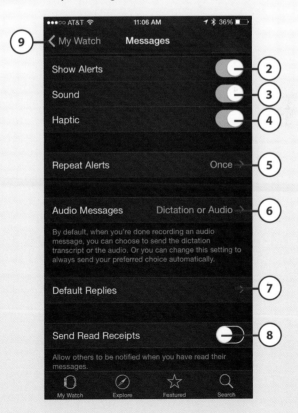

Music

Use these settings to decide if you want the Music app to show in the list of Glances, choose what playlist of music to synchronize to your Watch, and set a limit on the number of songs to synchronize from your chosen playlist.

1. Tap Show in Glances to choose whether you want the Music app to show in the list of Glances.

2. Tap Synced Playlist to choose a playlist of music on your iPhone that you want to synchronize to your Watch. When a playlist of music is synchronized to your Watch, you can play the songs in the playlist directly from your Watch, even when your iPhone is out of range.

3. Tap to choose how many songs should synchronize from your chosen playlist. You can set the limit by size (number of gigabytes) or number of songs.

4. Tap My Watch to save your changes and return to the previous screen.

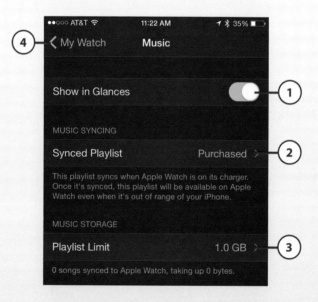

>>>*Go Further*

WHY PLAY MUSIC FROM YOUR WATCH?

Synchronizing music to your Watch allows you to play that music even when your iPhone is not in range. For example, when you go for a run, you can leave your iPhone behind, but still have the ability to listen to music as you exercise. Later in the book, there is a task explaining how to pair a Bluetooth headset or speaker to your Watch. You can play the songs you have synchronized directly from your Watch, or you can play them directly from your Watch on a Bluetooth-connected headset or speaker and enjoy much better sound quality.

Wallet and Apple Pay

Apple Pay on your Watch doesn't contain the same cards that you might have already added to your iPhone. Use these settings to manage the cards you want to use for Apple Pay on your Watch, and choose whether you want to be alerted by Apple Pay and Wallet on your Watch.

1. Tap Mirror my iPhone to have the Wallet and Apple Pay alerts on your Watch mirror how you have them set up on your iPhone, or you can tap Custom to choose settings specific to your Watch. If you chose Mirror my iPhone, skip to step 4.

2. Tap Add Credit or Debit Card to add a new card to Apple Pay on your Watch. For more information about adding cards to Apple Pay, turn to Chapter 6, "Using Apple Pay."

3. Tap Add next to one of the credit or debit cards that you have already added to your iPhone, to add that card to your Watch.

4. Tap Default Card to choose the default card to use for Apple Pay from your Watch, if you have added more than one card (not shown).

5. Tap My Watch to save your changes and return to the previous screen.

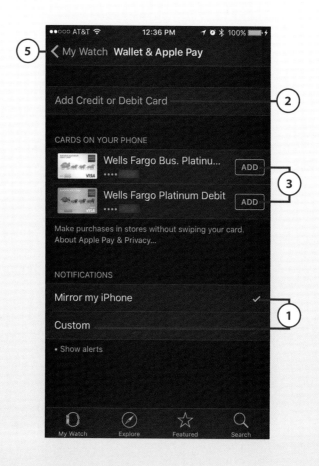

Phone

Choose to mirror how the Phone app alerts you on your Watch with how you have it set up on your iPhone, and control how you are alerted when the phone is ringing.

1. Tap Mirror my iPhone to have the Phone alerts on your Watch mirror how you have them set up on your iPhone, or tap Custom to choose settings specific to your Watch. If you chose Mirror my iPhone, skip to step 5.

2. Tap Show Alerts to choose whether you want to show alerts for missed calls and voicemails on your Watch. If you turn this off, skip to step 5.

3. Tap Sound to choose whether a sound is played when you are alerted of missed calls and voicemails.

4. Tap Haptic to choose whether you should feel a tap on your wrist when you are alerted of missed calls and voicemails.

5. Tap Sound to choose whether a sound is played while your iPhone is ringing.

6. Tap Haptic to choose whether you should feel repeated tapping on your wrist while your iPhone is ringing.

7. Tap My Watch to save your changes and return to the previous screen.

Photos

Use these settings to choose how the Photos app alerts you on your Watch and what photo album you want to synchronize to your Watch.

1. Tap Mirror my iPhone to have the Photos alerts on your Watch for iCloud sharing events mirror how you have them set up on your iPhone. Alternatively, you can tap Custom to choose settings specific to your Watch. If you chose Mirror my iPhone, skip to step 3.

2. Tap Show Alerts to choose whether you want to show alerts for iCloud sharing events on your Watch.

3. Tap Synced Album to choose which photo album on your iPhone you want to synchronize to your Watch.

4. Tap Photos Limit to choose how many photos from the chosen photo album you want to synchronize to your Watch.

5. Tap My Watch to save your changes and return to the previous screen.

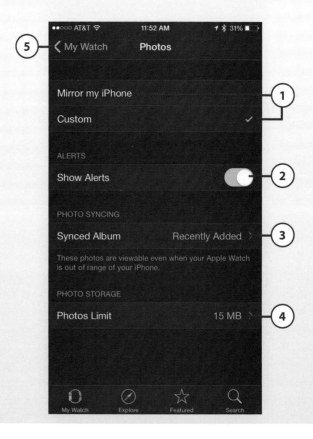

Stocks

Use these settings to decide whether the Stocks app appears in the Glances list, change the default stock, and choose the value to display for a given stock.

1. Tap Show in Glances to choose whether the Stocks app appears in the Glances list.

2. Tap Default Stock to choose the default stock shown when you look at the Stocks Glance, or when you use the Stocks complication on a watch face. You can leave it the same as the default stock you have chosen on your iPhone, or you can choose a different stock to show on your Watch.

3. Choose what value is shown when you use the Stocks complication on a watch face.

4. Tap My Watch to save your changes and return to the previous screen.

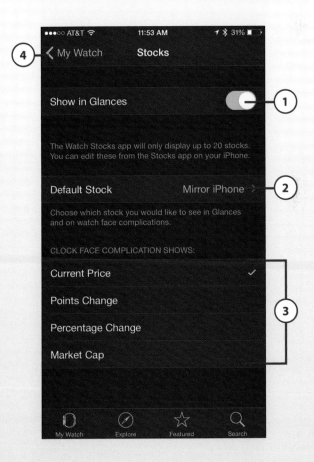

Weather

Use these settings to choose whether the Weather app appears in the Glances list and to change the default city for which the weather is shown.

1. Tap Default City to choose the default city for which the weather is shown when you look at the Weather Glance, or when you use the Weather complication on a watch face. You choose Current City, which uses your geographic location to figure out what city you are currently in, or you can choose a specific city. The list of cities you can choose from to display weather for can be edited in the Weather app on your iPhone.

2. Tap My Watch to save your changes and return to the previous screen.

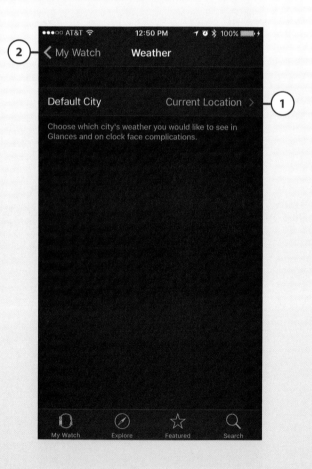

Workout

Use these settings to decide whether the Workout app shows information using numeric values or using the ring graphic, and decide whether to save additional battery life by not measuring your heart rate during running or walking workouts.

1. Tap Show Goal Metric to choose whether the Workout app shows your distance, calories burned, and elapsed time metrics as numeric values instead of using the progress ring during workouts.

2. Tap Power Saving Mode to save additional battery life by not measuring your heart rate during walking or running workouts.

3. Tap Pace View to choose wheter you want to see the current pace, or the pace average while you are working out.

4. Tap My Watch to save your changes and return to the previous screen.

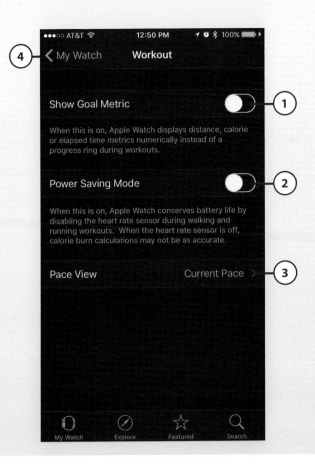

Change Settings for Third-Party Watch Apps

You can choose whether a third-party Watch app should be installed on your Watch. In some cases, additional settings can be chosen, such as choosing to show the app in the Glances list if the app supports Glances.

1. In the Apple Watch app on your iPhone, tap a third-party app. The list of apps shown here are all Watch apps that are available to use based on the apps you have installed on your iPhone. Any iPhone app that includes a Watch app is shown in this list. Tap an app to configure its settings.

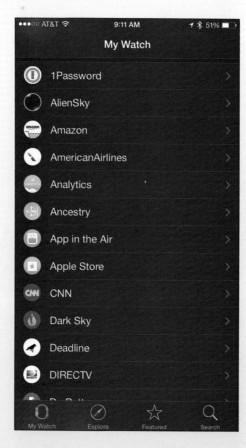

Scroll down to see all available Watch apps

2. Tap Show App on Apple Watch to choose whether you want to have this Watch app installed on your Watch.

3. Tap Show in Glances to choose whether you want this app to be shown in the Glances list. Not all Watch apps support Glances.

4. Tap My Watch to save your changes and return to the previous screen.

Take a call on your watch

In this chapter, you learn how to send and receive messages, read and act upon emails, and use the phone from your Watch. Topics include the following:

→ Sending and receiving messages
→ Using Digital Touch
→ Reading and replying to emails
→ Making and receiving phone calls

2

Messages, Emails, and Phone Calls

Your Apple Watch provides a rich experience that allows you to send and receive messages (SMS, MMS, and iMessages) using the Messages app, read and act upon emails, and use your Watch as a speaker phone.

Working with Messages

Your Apple Watch allows you to send and receive Short Message Service (SMS) messages, Multimedia Message Service (MMS) messages, and iMessages. You can also send and receive a special type of messaging called Digital Touch when you communicate with other Apple Watch users.

Read and Respond to Messages from Notifications

When you receive a new message, you can read it, reply to it, or dismiss it from your Apple Watch.

1. Raise your wrist when you feel a tap to see the notification for a new message. If you don't raise your wrist immediately, you can still interact with the message by swiping down from the top of the Watch screen to see unread notifications.

2. Turn the Digital Crown or swipe up on the watch face to scroll through the message. When you reach the bottom of the message, you see the Reply button.

3. Tap Reply to reply to the message. You can also tap Dismiss to dismiss the message.

4. Turn the Digital Crown to scroll through the list of default replies you can choose to reply with. You can also dictate a response or respond with an emoji. See the two tasks that follow for instructions on using those responses.

5. Tap the quick response, and it will be sent as your reply.

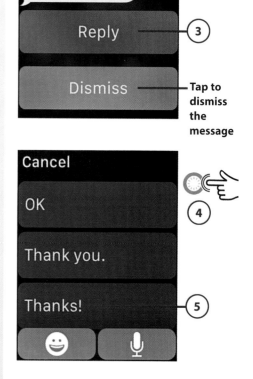

Tap to dismiss the message

Dictate Your Response

If none of the default replies are appropriate to respond with, you can dictate a response. Follow steps 1–3 in the previous section "Read and Respond to Messages from Notifications" and then continue with the steps that follow.

1. Tap the microphone icon to dictate your response to the message.

2. Dictate your response to the message after you see the dictation screen appear.

3. Tap Done when you are ready to send the dictated message.

4. Tap the visualization of your audio to send your response as an audio recording.

5. Tap the translation of your dictated response to send your response as text.

6. Tap Cancel if you want to cancel the reply and try again.

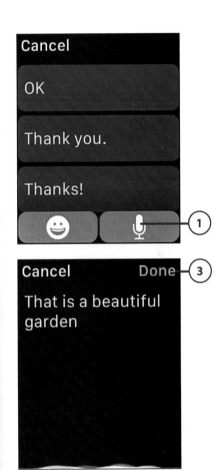

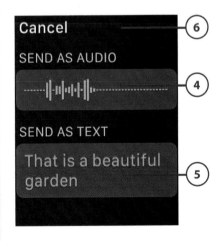

Respond Using an Emoji

Your Apple Watch can send regular
emojis as well as special animated
emojis only found on the Apple
Watch. Follow steps 1–3 in the previous section "Read and Respond to
Messages from Notifications" and
then continue with the steps that
follow.

1. Tap the emoji icon.

2. Turn the Digital Crown to scroll
   through all the animated face
   emojis. If you find one you want
   to use, tap Send to send it.

3. If you don't want to use a face
   emoji, swipe from right to left
   to move to the next type of
   animated emoji.

4. Turn the Digital Crown to scroll
   through all the animated heart
   emojis. If you find one you want
   to use, tap Send to send it.

5. If you don't want to use a heart
   emoji, swipe from right to left
   to move to the next type of
   animated emoji.

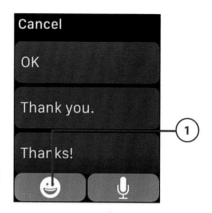

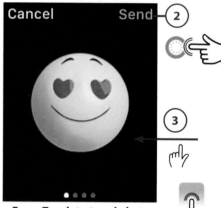

**Force Touch to toggle between
yellow and red faces**

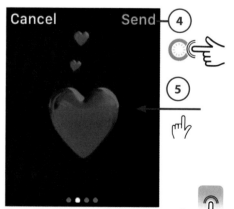

**Force Touch to toggle between red,
blue, and purple hearts**

6. Turn the Digital Crown to scroll through all the animated hand emojis. If you find one you want to use, tap Send to send it.

7. If you don't want to use a hand emoji, swipe from right to left to move to the list of your frequently used regular emoji.

8. Turn the Digital Crown to scroll through all your frequently used regular non-animated emojis. If you find one you want to use, tap it to send it. The list of frequently used emojis comes from your iPhone.

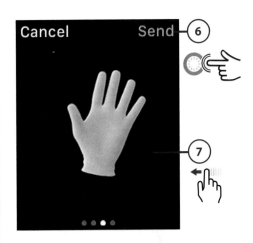

Change the Color of Face and Heart Animated Emojis

If you Force Touch while choosing the animated face emojis, you toggle between the yellow face and the red face. If you Force Touch while choosing the animated heart emoji, you can cycle through red, blue, and purple heart colors.

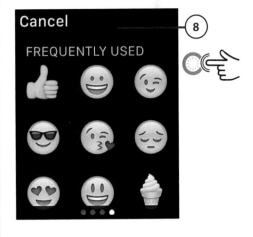

Read and Respond to Messages from the Messages App

If you want to see all your messages from all senders, you can use the Messages app.

1. Raise your wrist and press the Digital Crown to see the Home screen.

2. Tap the Message app icon.

3. Turn the Digital Crown to scroll through the list of senders.

4. Tap a sender to read all messages sent by that person.

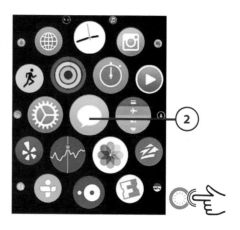

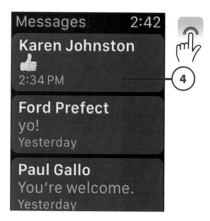

5. Turn the Digital Crown to scroll up and down the list of messages.

6. Tap Reply if you would like to compose a reply to the sender.

>>>Go Further

SEE SENDER DETAILS AND SEND YOUR LOCATION

If you Force Touch the watch face while reading a message, you get access to several options. You can tap Reply to respond to the message. You can tap Details to see all details about the sender of the message, as long as you have the sender in your Contacts already. You can tap Send Location to send your current location to that contact.

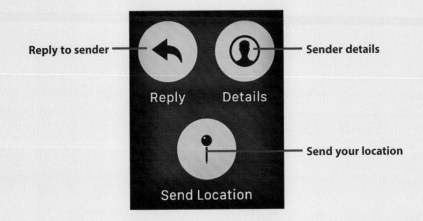

Compose a New Message from the Messages App

Most of the time you will use the Side Button to quickly send messages to your favorite contacts, but while you have the Messages app open, you can go ahead and compose a new message.

1. Press the Digital Crown to see the Home screen.

2. Tap the Messages app icon.

3. Force Touch on the watch face.

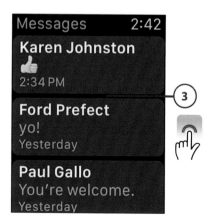

4. Tap New Message.

5. Tap Add Contact to add a recipient for your message.

6. Tap one of the contacts you communicate with often, or tap the microphone icon and speak the name of the contact you want to add. If the contact is not one you communicate with often, tap the blue contact icon to choose that contact from your full contact list.

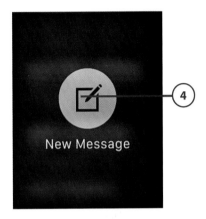

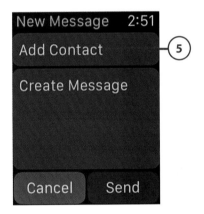

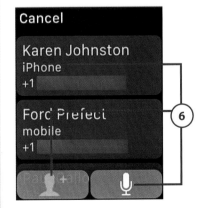

7. Tap Create Message.

8. Choose to use either a quick response or an emoji, or you can dictate your message.

9. Tap Send to send the message.

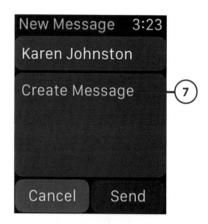

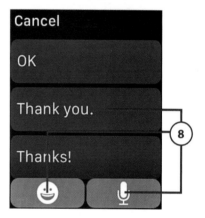

Compose a New Message from the Friends List

Your Apple Watch has a Side Button that accesses your Friends list. This enables you to very quickly communicate with your favorite people. Here is how to use that feature to quickly send a text message.

1. Press the Side Button to be immediately taken to the list of your favorite people.

2. Turn the Digital Crown to choose the person you want to send a message to. After you have them selected, wait a second and the screen advances to the Phone and Messages icons, or tap their picture to go immediately to that screen.

3. Tap the Messages icon.

4. Choose to either use a default reply as your message, dictate a message, or send an emoji.

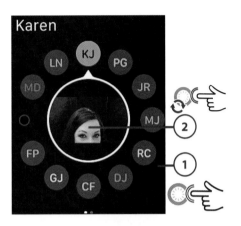

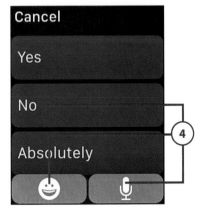

>>>*Go Further*

HAND OFF A MESSAGE TO YOUR iPHONE OR iMAC

If you start composing a new message, or start replying to a message, on your Watch, you can continue with the message on your iPhone or Mac. As you use the Messages app, your iPhone and Mac get ready to take over the message by displaying the Messages app icon. On your iPhone, you see a Messages icon in the bottom-left corner of the lock screen, and on your Mac you see a Message Handoff icon just to the left of the Dock. If you want to continue the message on your iPhone, press the Home button and then swipe the Messages icon up. If you have set a passcode to unlock your iPhone, or you use Touch ID to unlock your iPhone, you are prompted to do that. Once you unlock your iPhone, the Messages app launches and displays the message you were working on, allowing you to continue with it. If you want to continue the message on your Mac, click the Message Handoff icon to the left of the Dock. The Messages app launches and displays the message you were working on, allowing you to continue with it. For Handoff to work, your Watch and iPhone must be on the same Wi-Fi network (this is typical). For Handoff to work with your Mac, your Watch and Mac must be on the same Wi-Fi network (this is not typical unless you are at home).

Start a message on your Watch —

Swipe the Messages icon up to continue on your iPhone

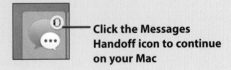

Click the Messages Handoff icon to continue on your Mac

Using Digital Touch

In addition to SMS, MMS, and iMessages, you can use a special kind of communication called Digital Touch. Digital Touch only works with contacts who have their own Apple Watch. You can send or receive a tap pattern, a sketch, or a heartbeat.

Send a Digital Touch

Choose a color and tap or draw a sketch, and if you want to, send your real heartbeat to someone else wearing an Apple Watch.

1. Press the Side Button to see the people in your Friends app.

2. Turn the Digital Crown to choose one of your friends who has an Apple Watch.

3. Tap the Digital Touch icon. Only friends who wear an Apple Watch have this icon available.

4. Hold two fingers on the screen for a few seconds to start sending your real heartbeat. Keep holding two fingers on the screen to continue sending your heartbeat. Lift your fingers to stop sending your heartbeat. If you don't want to send your heartbeat, skip to step 5.

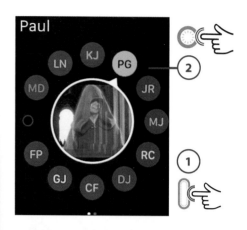

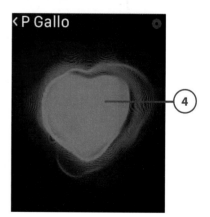

5. Tap the color icon to choose a color to use to draw a sketch or do a tap pattern.

6. Tap the color that you want to use to draw a sketch or to tap out a pattern with.

7. Tap a sequence on the screen. Each time you tap, a visual tap impression is left on the screen using the color your chose. The sequence of taps is sent to your friend wearing an Apple Watch.

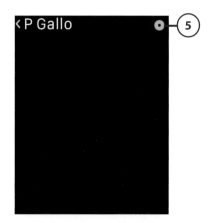

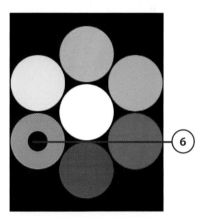

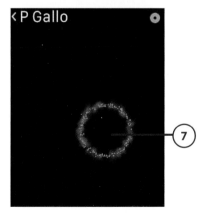

8. Use your finger to draw a sketch on the screen. The sketch can be as simple or as complex as you like. After you have finished your sketch, wait a couple of seconds and the sketch is sent.

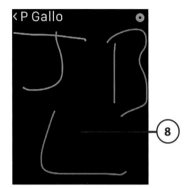

Multiple Colors for Sketches

You can draw sketches using more than one color. To do this, after you have finished using the one color, tap the color pick icon again, choose a new color, and continue sketching.

Receive a Digital Touch

When you receive a Digital Touch, you feel a tap on your wrist, and you are prompted to view it.

1. Raise your wrist after you feel the notification tap.

2. Read the screen to see what kind of Digital Touch has been sent. In this example, it is a sketch. The screen will automatically change to "Tap to view."

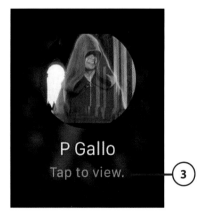

3. Tap the notification to view the Digital Touch. The Digital Touch starts. If the Digital Touch is a sketch, you see the sketch being drawn. If it is a tap pattern, you feel the taps on your wrist and see the visual tap on the screen. If it is a heartbeat, you feel the sender's actual heartbeat as taps on your wrist.

4. Tap the Play button to replay the Digital Touch.

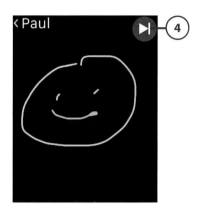

Working with Email

Your Apple Watch enables you to read emails and take actions on them, including marking the email as unread, flagging the email, deleting or archiving it, and replying to it.

Read Email from Within a Notification

When you receive a new email, you can read it and take certain actions on it.

1. Raise your wrist, when you feel a tap, to see the notification for a new email. If you don't raise your wrist immediately, you can still interact with the email by swiping down from the top of the Watch screen to see unread notifications.

2. Turn the Digital Crown to scroll through the email.

3. Tap to reply to the email.

4. Tap to mark the email as unread.

5. Tap to flag the email.

6. Tap to archive or delete the email. This action is Archive for Gmail and Delete for all other email account types.

7. Tap to dismiss the notification.

Reply To Email from Within a Notification

New! With Watch OS 2.0, you can now reply to an email using your Watch. You can reply using emoji, using a default reply, or by dictating a reply. Follow steps 1–3 in the previous section, "Read Email from Within a Notification," and then continue with the steps that follow.

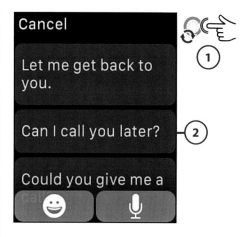

1. Turn the Digital Crown to scroll through the list of default replies you can choose to respond with.

2. Tap the default reply you want to use.

3. Tap Send to send your reply.

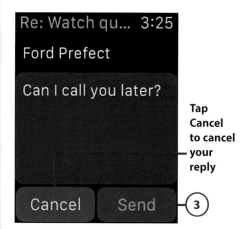

Tap Cancel to cancel your reply

Dictate Your Response

New! If none of the default replies are appropriate to respond with, you can dictate a response. Follow steps 1–3 in the previous section "Read Email from Within a Notification" and then continue with the steps that follow.

1. Tap the microphone icon to dictate your response to the message.

2. Dictate your response to the message after you see the dictation screen appear.

3. Tap Done when you are ready to send the dictated message.

4. Tap Send to send your reply.

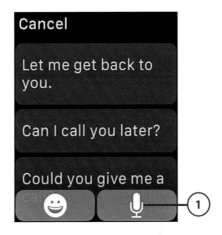

Tap Cancel to cancel your reply

Respond Using an Emoji

New! If you would like to just send an emoji as a reply, you can. Follow steps 1–3 in the previous section "Read Email from Within a Notification," and then continue with the steps that follow.

1. Tap the emoji icon.

2. Turn the Digital Crown to scroll through all your frequently-used, non-animated emojis. The list of frequently used emojis comes from your iPhone. If you scroll further down, you will see all available emojis.

3. Tap an emoji.

4. Tap Send to send your reply.

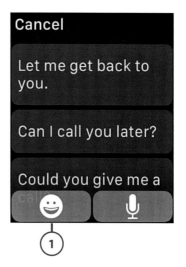

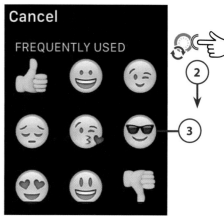

Receiving Multiple Email Notifications

If you do not look at your notifications right away, and you receive more than one email, when you look at the notification it does not show the actual email. Rather, it shows a notification telling you how many messages you have received and from whom. If you tap on that notification, it expands to show all email notifications separately. Tap each email notification to read the email.

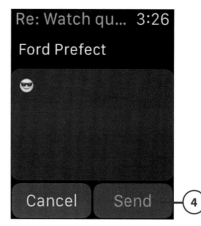

>>>Go Further

HAND OFF AN EMAIL TO YOUR iPHONE OR MAC

If you start replying to an email on your Watch, you can continue with the message on your iPhone or Mac. As you use the Mail app, your iPhone and Mac get ready to take over the email by displaying the Mail app icon. On your iPhone, you see the Mail icon in the bottom-left corner of the lock screen, and on your Mac you see a Mail Handoff icon just to the left of the Dock. If you want to continue the email on your iPhone, press the Home button, and then swipe the Mail icon up. If you have set a passcode to unlock your iPhone, or you use Touch ID to unlock your iPhone, you are prompted to do that. After you unlock your iPhone, the Mail app launches and displays the email you were working on, allowing you to continue with it. If you want to continue the email on your Mac, click the Mail Handoff icon to the left of the Dock. The Mail app launches and displays the email you were working on, allowing you to continue with it. For Handoff to work with your iPhone, your Watch and iPhone must be on the same Wi-Fi network (this is typical). For Handoff to work with your Mac, your Watch and Mac must be on the same Wi-Fi network. (This is not typical unless you are at home or in an office on a Wi-Fi network.)

Swipe the Mail icon up to continue on your iPhone

Click the Mail Handoff icon to continue on your Mac

Use the Mail App

Although you can quickly interact with incoming emails from the notification as they arrive, you can also use the Mail app to see all emails in your inbox, read them, and take actions on them.

1. Press the Digital Crown to see the Home screen.

2. Tap the Mail app.

3. Turn the Digital Crown to scroll through all of the emails.

4. Tap an email to read it.

5. Force Touch while reading an email to see actions you can take on that email.

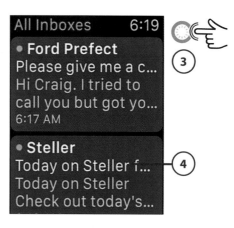

Call or Map from an Email

As you scroll through an email on your Apple Watch, if you see a phone number, you can tap it to place a call to the number shown. If you see an address, you can tap it to show that address in the Maps app. While it is shown in the Maps app, you can also get turn-by-turn directions to the address.

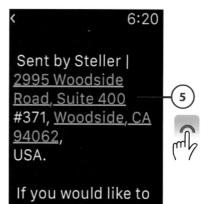

6. Tap Reply to reply to the email using either of the methods explained in the previous tasks.

7. Tap Flag to flag the email. After the email is flagged, you return to the list of emails.

8. Tap Unread to mark the email as unread. After the email is marked as unread, you return to the list of emails.

9. Tap Archive (or Trash) to archive or delete the email. This action archives Gmail messages and deletes the message for all other email account types. After the email is deleted, you return to the list of emails.

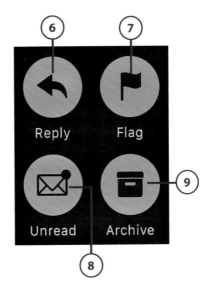

>>>Go Further

TAKE ACTIONS ON AN EMAIL BEFORE YOU OPEN IT

You can archive or delete an email, flag it, or mark it as unread before you open it. To do this, swipe the email from right to left. Tap Archive (or Trash) to archive Gmail or delete other types of email. Tap More. You can flag the email with a colored dot or flag shape, depending what you chose in your Apple Watch app settings for Mail. Tap "Mark as unread" to mark that message as unread. This option becomes "Mark as read" if the message is currently unread.

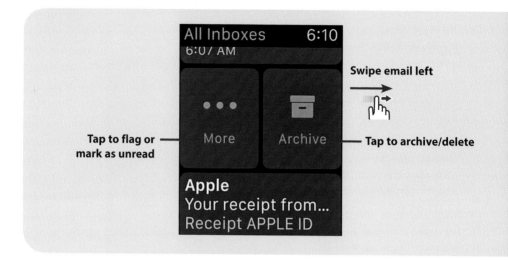

Tap to flag or mark as unread

Swipe email left

Tap to archive/delete

Make and Receive Phone Calls

Your Apple Watch allows you to make or answer phone calls right on your wrist. If you decide to answer or make a call on your Watch, bear in mind the background noise in your environment greatly affects the clarity of the call for both you and the person on the other end.

Handle an Incoming Call

When someone calls you, you see the incoming call notification on your Watch, and you can answer or decline the call.

1. Raise your wrist when you feel repeated tapping to see the incoming call notification.

2. Tap the red phone icon to decline the call and send it to voicemail.

3. Tap the green phone icon to answer the call on your Watch.

4. Turn the Digital Crown to scroll down when a call is coming in and you see two additional options. You can tap Send a Message to reject the call but send a quick message to the caller via SMS (or iMessage, if they are also an iPhone or Apple Watch user). You see a few predefined responses to use, but you can also send emoji, and even speak a custom response message.

5. You can tap Answer on iPhone to answer the call on your iPhone instead of your Apple Watch.

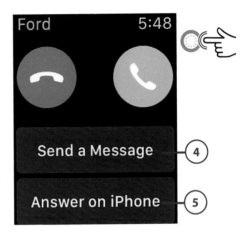

>>>Go Further
TAKING THE CALL ON YOUR iPHONE

When you choose the option to take an incoming call on your iPhone, what actually happens is that the call is answered but immediately put on hold. The caller hears an on-hold tone while you pick up your iPhone and swipe to answer the call. The call then transfers to your iPhone and the call comes off hold. While the call is on hold, your Watch shows a screen that allows you to hang up, or you can tap an icon that makes your iPhone play a loud sound and illuminate the camera flash, if you are having trouble finding it.

Options During a Call

If you choose to answer the call on your Apple Watch, during the call you can adjust the volume and mute your audio.

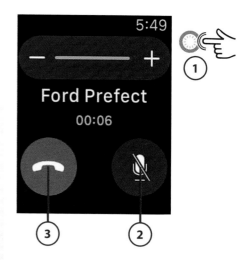

1. Turn the Digital Crown, or tap the + and – buttons, to adjust the volume.

2. Tap the mute icon to mute or unmute your audio.

3. Tap the red phone icon to end the call.

Use the Phone App

In addition to quickly interacting with incoming calls, you can also use the Phone app to see and call your favorite contacts, see recent calls, view all your contacts and call them, and play back voicemails.

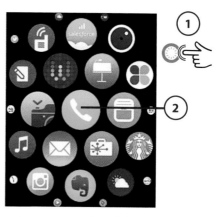

1. Press the Digital Crown to see the Home screen.

2. Tap the Phone app.

3. Tap Favorites to see your favorite contacts.

4. Tap Recents to see recent missed, incoming, and outgoing calls.

5. Tap Contacts to see all your contacts.

6. Tap Voicemail to see your voice-mails and play them back.

Use Your Favorites

If you have designated any contacts as favorites on your iPhone, those same favorites are available in the Phone app on your Watch.

1. Turn the Digital Crown to scroll through the list of your favorites.

2. Tap a favorite to call them.

3. Tap Favorites to return to the main Phone app screen.

How Do I Add Favorites?

You can add or manage your favorites on your iPhone. To do this, tap the Phone icon and then tap Favorites. To add a favorite, tap the add icon (plus symbol) and choose a contact. If the contact you chose has more than one phone number, tap the number you want to use to call them when calling using the Favorites feature. Your changes will appear on your Watch.

Manage Recent Calls

The Recents screen shows you all recent outgoing, incoming, and missed calls. Tapping a recent call places a call to the number or person shown.

1. Turn the Digital Crown to scroll through the list of your recent calls.

2. Tap a recent call to place a call to the number or person shown.

3. Tap Recents to return to the main Phone app screen.

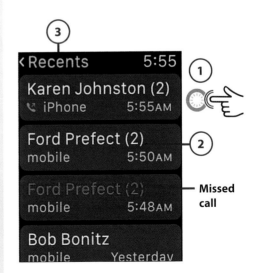

Place a Call from Your Contacts

The Contacts screen shows you all contacts you have in the Contacts app on your iPhone. You can find a contact, call them, or send them a message.

1. Turn the Digital Crown to scroll through all your contacts. Scrolling quickly through your contacts switches the scroll view to scrolling by letter. When the letter you want is shown, stop scrolling.

2. Tap the contact you want to call.

3. Tap the phone icon to call the contact.

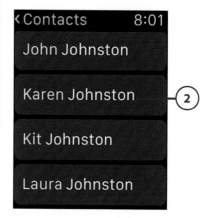

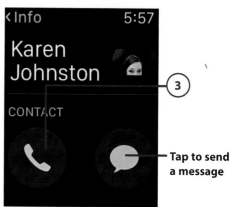

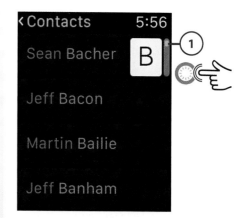

Tap to send a message

4. If the contact has more than one phone number, tap the number you want to call.

Manage Voicemail

The Voicemail screen shows you all of your voicemail and allows you to play each voicemail and delete it.

1. Turn the Digital Crown to scroll through all of your voicemail.

2. Tap a voicemail message to listen to it. If it is a new message that you have not yet played, it immediately starts playing.

3. Turn the Digital Crown to adjust the volume of the audio.

4. Tap to pause the voicemail playback. Tap again to resume playback.

5. Tap to skip back 5 seconds.

6. Tap to skip ahead 5 seconds.

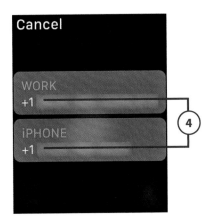

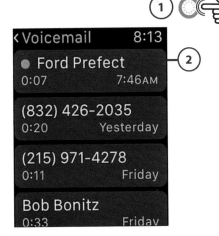

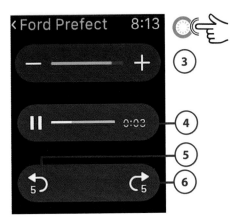

7. Tap to replay the voicemail.

8. Tap the green phone icon to call the person who left the voicemail.

9. Tap the red trash can icon to delete the voicemail.

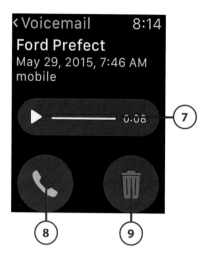

Listen to a Voicemail from a Notification

When you receive a notification on your Watch that you have a new voicemail, you can play the voicemail directly from the notification. If you use the Digital Crown to scroll down below the play icon, you can call the person back, send them a message, or dismiss the voicemail notification.

>>>Go Further

MAKING A CALL USING THE FRIENDS APP

A quick way to call one of your friends is to use the Friends app. To do this, press the Side Button to see your friends. Turn the Digital Crown to choose the friends you want to call. Either wait 2 seconds or tap the friend's picture. Tap the phone icon to place a call to them. If they have more than one phone number, you are prompted to choose the number to call.

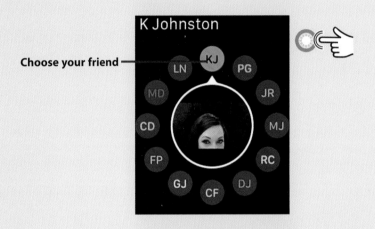

Choose your friend

Tap to call

Ask Siri to set a reminder for you

In this chapter, you learn how to use Siri, your iPhone and Apple Watch's personal digital assistant, to help you call people, set reminders, and generally help you use your Watch more efficiently. Topics include the following:

→ Learning how to activate Siri
→ Using Siri to achieve tasks on your Watch
→ Handing off Siri to your iPhone for more complicated tasks

Using Siri

Your Apple Watch includes Siri, the same personal digital assistant found on your iPhone. You can use Siri to initiate phone calls, set reminders, send messages, set alarms, and generally help out getting things done using your Watch.

Activating Siri

There are two ways to activate Siri, depending on how you have set up your Apple Watch. The tasks that follow look at both ways.

Raise Your Wrist

You can activate Siri by raising your wrist.

1. Raise your wrist and say, "Hey Siri."

2. Siri activates, and you feel a tap on your wrist. The words "Hey Siri..." appear at the top of the screen, and you see sound waves at the bottom of the screen.

3. Speak a command to Siri, such as "Conference call with Craig today at 1 p.m."

Hey Siri

2

Press the Digital Crown

You can activate Siri by pressing the Digital Crown.

1. Press and hold the Digital Crown.

2. Siri activates, and you feel a tap on your wrist. You see the words "What can I help you with?" at the top of the screen, and you see sound waves at the bottom of the screen.

3. Stop pressing the Digital Crown and speak a command to Siri, such as "Where is the closest gas station?"

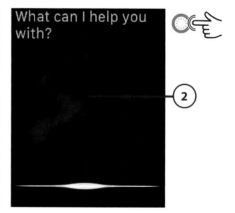

What can I help you with?

2

Using Siri

Once Siri has activated, you can ask her to perform tasks for you or ask her for information.

Time-Related Requests

You can use Siri to set and manage alarms, timers, calendar events, and reminders as well as ask her time-related questions. If you want to set up calendar events and reminders in one step rather than several, be as specific as you can. Instead of saying, "New event at 4 p.m. tomorrow," you should say, "Meet with Doctor Mason tomorrow at 4 p.m." Otherwise, the new event is given the default title of "Event" and you'll have to ask Siri to edit the event to add the title, or you can do it manually on your iPhone later.

Managing Alarms

Ask Siri to set and manage alarms for you.

1. Activate Siri and say, "Set an alarm for 2 p.m."

2. Siri creates a new alarm and shows it on the screen.

3. Alternatively, you can say to Siri, "Wake me up in 6 hours."

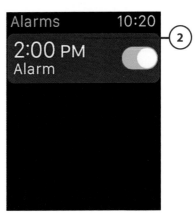

4. Siri creates a new alarm for 6 hours from now and shows it on the screen.

5. To cancel one of your alarms, tell Siri, "Cancel my 2 p.m. alarm."

6. Siri turns off your alarm and shows it on the screen.

Managing Reminders

You can ask Siri to set reminders for you. The subject of the reminder can be anything you want.

1. Tell Siri to "set a reminder to call Mom tomorrow." You could also be more time specific and tell Siri to "set a reminder to call Mom tomorrow at 10 a.m."

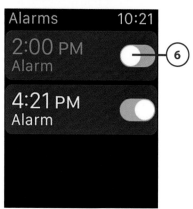

2. Tap OK to accept the reminder that Siri creates.

3. If you decide that you don't want to set the reminder, use the Digital Crown to scroll down and tap Cancel (not shown).

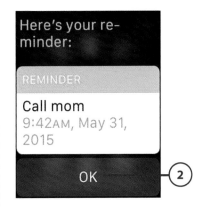

Managing Timers

You can ask Siri to set and manage timers for you.

1. Tell Siri to "set a timer for 2 minutes" (not shown).

2. Siri creates a timer for 2 minutes and starts the countdown.

3. You can either leave the timer countdown on the screen and interact with it by tapping the Cancel or Pause button, or press the Digital Crown to go back to the watch face view and let the timer count down in the background.

4. While the timer is counting down, but not visible on your Watch screen, you can activate Siri and tell her to "show my timer," "pause timer," "resume timer," or "stop timer."

Managing Calendar Events

You can ask Siri to create or edit calendar events for you, and ask her event related questions.

1. Ask Siri to "create a meeting with Karen tomorrow at 9 a.m." If you have more than one contact with the same name, or the contact has more than one email address, Siri asks you to clarify who the correct contact is and/or which email address before continuing. You can also ask Siri to schedule a recurring meeting by saying, "Create a meeting every Friday about status reports."

2. Siri creates the new event for you and shows the information about the event on the screen. If you have a conflict, Siri asks if you want to schedule the event anyway. You can confirm or cancel the event at that point.

3. You can ask Siri event-related questions such as, "What does the rest of my day look like?" or "What's on my calendar for Monday?" You can also ask Siri, "When am I meeting with Karen?"

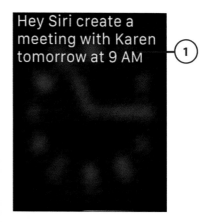

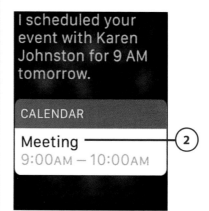

Ask Siri Time-Related Questions

You can ask Siri questions about time in other cities, or what day certain holidays fall on.

1. Ask Siri, "What time is it in Cape Town?"

2. Siri shows you the current time in Cape Town and the number of hours ahead of your time zone it is.

3. You can ask Siri, "What's the date next Saturday?"

4. Siri shows the date.

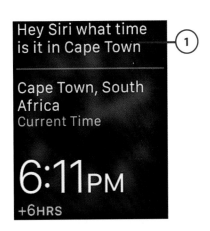

Informational Requests

You can use Siri to get information such as sports scores, stock information, weather information, and movie times.

Ask Siri for Sports-Related Information

You can ask Siri many sports-related questions, including team scores, best rated teams, when a game will be played, and many more.

1. Tell Siri, "Show me soccer scores from last night." Siri shows the scores between teams that played last night.

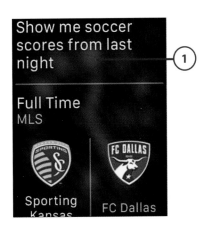

2. Ask Siri, "Who's the best team in ice hockey?" Siri shows the results.

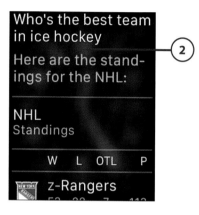

Ask Siri for Weather, Stocks, and General Information

You can ask Siri about the weather, stocks you follow, your schedule, and general information, and ask her to find images on the Internet.

1. Ask Siri, "Will I need my umbrella tomorrow?" Siri lets you know if you do and shows you the weekly forecast.

2. Ask Siri, "What's the temperature in Durban, South Africa?" Siri shows you the temperature and current conditions.

3. Ask Siri, "What is Apple's stock price?" Siri shows you the stock information.

4. Tell Siri, "Show me my calendar."

5. Siri launches the Calendar app for you and shows the current day in Day or Today mode, depending on which one you chose last time you were in the Calendar app.

6. Ask Siri, "What is the square root of 128?" Siri shows the results.

7. Tell Siri, "Show me pictures of Capital Radio 604." Siri shows pictures matching your search term.

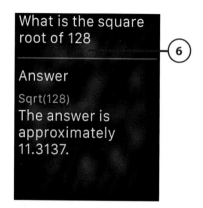

Launch Apps Using Siri

You can ask Siri to launch apps on your Watch. For example, you can ask Siri to "open Mail" to open the Mail app, or "launch Workout" to open the Workout app. Instead of asking Siri to launch the Workout app, you can be more specific. For example, you can say "Hey Siri, start a run" or "Hey Siri, start a 200 calorie indoor bike ride."

View Glances Using Siri

You can ask Siri to open any of your Glances. For example, you can say "Hey Siri, show my heart beat glance," or "Hey Siri, check the battery."

>>>Go Further

HANDING OFF SIRI TO YOUR iPHONE

In some situations, you might ask Siri to do something that it can do, but only on your iPhone. One example is asking Siri to identify the song that's playing. Ask Siri, "What song is playing?" She tells you to use Handoff to let your iPhone handle the request. On your iPhone, swipe up on the microphone icon to hand off Siri to your iPhone. Siri on your iPhone identifies the song playing.

Siri asks you to use Handoff

Siri listens to the song

20:54 ETA   20:51

Perimeter
Mall

285

Clear   Start

Turn-by-turn
directions

In this chapter, you learn how to use the Maps app on your Apple Watch to find places around you and navigate using turn-by-turn directions. Topics include the following:

→ Find places around you

→ Map addresses from your contacts

→ Get turn-by-turn directions

→ Hand off Maps to your iPhone

→ Use Transit Directions

Using Apple Maps

Your Apple Watch includes the Maps app. Like the Maps app on your iPhone, Maps on your Watch can provide information and turn-by-turn directions.

Launching Maps

You can launch the Maps app from the Home Screen.

1. Press the Digital Crown to show the Home Screen.

2. Tap the Maps app icon.

3. Tap the blue arrow to zoom in to your location.

4. Move around the map by swiping in any direction with your finger.

5. Turn the Digital Crown to zoom in and out of the map.

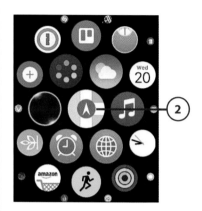

Just See Where You Are

If you just want to see your current location, use the Maps Glance. To do this, swipe up from the bottom of the Watch screen and then swipe left or right until you see the Maps Glance. Tap the map to launch the Maps app.

Search for a Place and Get Directions to It

You can search for a place using dictation, select from your list of favorite places, or choose from places you have recently visited.

1. Force Touch the watch face to see a list of actions.

2. Tap Search.

3. Tap Dictation to speak a person, place, type of destination, or a search term such as "find me pizza" or "where can I get lunch?" Tap one of the search results to select the place and then skip to step 6.

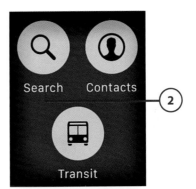

4. Tap Favorites to see a list of places you have marked as your favorites. Tap one of your favorite places and skip to step 6.

5. Tap one of the places you have recently been to. Turn the Digital Crown to scroll down to see all recent places. Proceed to step 6.

How Do I Add Favorites?

To manage your Maps favorites, when using Maps on your iPhone, you tap on a red pin (location you searched for) or blue dot (your current location), tap the Share icon, and then tap Add to Favorites. To remove a favorite, tap the search bar, tap Favorites, and then swipe left across a favorite to delete it.

Tap to call

6. Read the information about the place you have chosen, including ratings and operating hours, and then turn the Digital Crown to scroll down to choose whether you want driving or walking directions.

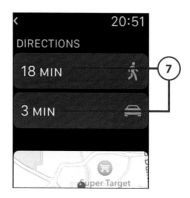

7. Tap to choose either walking or driving directions. In this example, we will use driving directions.

8. Tap Start to start the turn-by-turn directions.

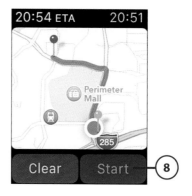

9. Follow the turn-by-turn directions on the screen.

10. If you would like to see the directions visually on the map, swipe right to left.

11. View the route and your current location on the map.

12. Swipe left to right to return to the text-only directions.

13. Follow the turn-by-turn directions to your destination. Your Watch taps your wrist a certain number of times to indicate a left or right turn. When you feel the taps, either take the turn or raise your wrist to see your next turn.

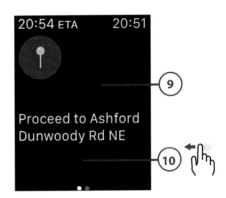

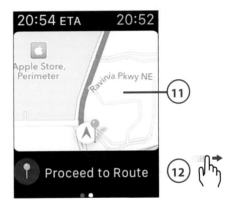

Learn the Navigation Taps

While your Watch is providing turn-by-turn directions, it uses a series of taps to direct you. If you feel three pairs of two taps, it means you must turn left at the intersection you are approaching. If you feel 12 taps in a row, it means turn right at the intersection you are approaching. If you feel a vibration, it means you are on the last leg of your journey. You also feel a vibration when you arrive at your destination.

Actions While Navigating

While your Watch is providing turn-by-turn directions, if you Force Touch, you can tap the X to cancel the turn-by-turn directions, or you can tap the phone icon to call the number for the place to which you are navigating.

Hand Off Directions Between Your iPhone and Watch

While you are using your Watch to get to your destination, you can use Handoff to let your iPhone take over. You can also use Handoff to let your Watch pick up from your iPhone. Handoff when using Maps is instant and doesn't require swiping up the Handoff icon.

1. After you have started the turn-by-turn directions on your Watch, pick up your iPhone and press the Home button.

2. The turn-by-turn directions appear right on the lock screen. Continue following the directions on your iPhone.

3. If you want to continue the directions on your Watch again, simply raise your wrist and continue following the directions.

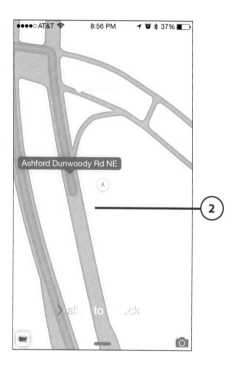

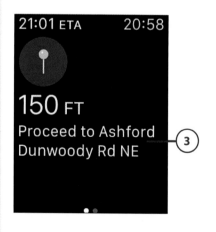

Stick a Pin in the Map

If you find a place while browsing the map, you can stick a pin into the map to mark the location.

1. Find a place that you would like to pin. Touch and hold on the place.

2. A pin is stuck into the map. Tap the pin to see information about the place, get walking or driving directions to it, or remove the pin.

3. Turn the Digital Crown to scroll up and down to see information about the place you have pinned.

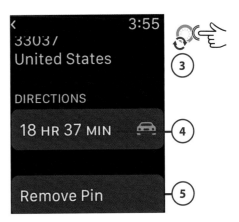

4. Tap to get walking or driving directions to the pinned place. In this example, only driving directions are available.

5. Tap Remove Pin to remove the pin.

Use a Pin to See an Address of Any Place

Sticking a pin in the map and then tapping it is a great way to get an address for anywhere on the map.

Get Directions to One of Your Contacts

You can get walking or driving directions to anyone you have in your Contacts, as long as you have an address entered for them.

1. Force Touch on the Map.

2. Tap Contacts. Turn the Digital Crown to scroll through your list of contacts.

3. Tap the person you want to get driving directions to.

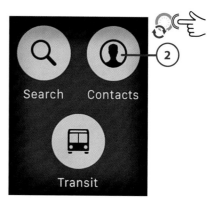

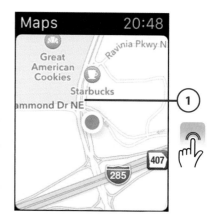

4. Turn the Digital Crown to scroll down through the information about the contact.

5. Tap the address of the contact.

6. Tap to choose walking or driving directions.

Tap to send a message

Tap to call

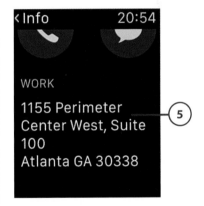

View Information About a Landmark

If you see a landmark on the map, such as a museum, train station, park, or monument, you can get information about that landmark as well as directions to it.

1. Tap the landmark.

2. Turn the Digital Crown to scroll through the information about the landmark. The information can include hours of operation, address, and phone number.

3. Tap walking or driving directions to get walking or driving directions to the landmark.

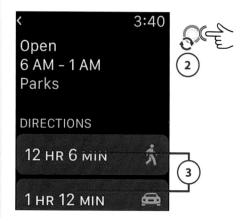

Get Transit Directions

New! In addition to walking and driving directions, you can get directions to a location using public transportation like busses, trains, and ferries.

1. Force Touch on the watch face to switch between Transit and Standard map views.

2. Tap Transit. The map displays bus and train stations.

3. Force Touch on the map.

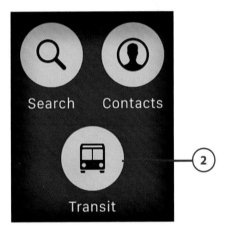

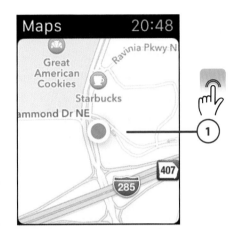

4. Tap Search or Contacts depending on how you want to find your destination.

5. Find a destination using Dictation, Favorites, or tap one of your recent destinations.

6. Tap Start.

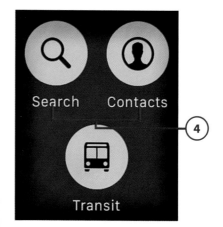

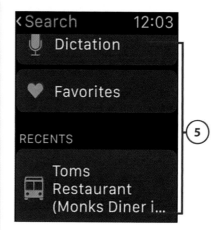

7. Your transit directions always start with a short walk to the public transportation entry point, in this case a subway station.

8. Turn the Digital Crown to move between the steps.

9. Continue following the steps instructing you to board specific trains.

10. When you are instructed to exit a ferry terminal, bus station, or train station, always pay attention to the exit you are being directed to.

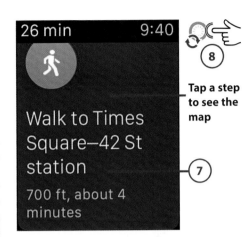

Tap a step to see the map

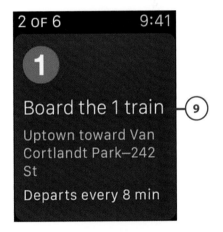

11. The last step of your transit directions always includes a short walk from the ferry terminal, bus station, or train station to your destination.

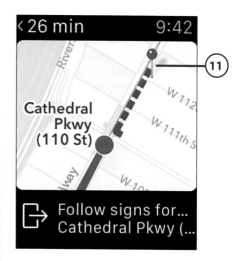

Transit Directions Cannot Include Driving Directions

Outside of major cities, when you want to get directions to a destination using public transportation, you must first use a separate driving or walking trip to arrive at the train, ferry, or bus station that you want to leave from. Then, you can create a new trip using public transportation to your final destination.

Choose where to play music from

See what's playing now

In this chapter, you learn how to use the Music app on your Watch to control music playback on your iPhone and directly from your Watch. Topics include the following:

→ Becoming familiar with the Music app
→ Controlling music playback
→ Connecting a Bluetooth headset or speaker
→ Playing music from your Watch

5

Playing Music

Your Apple Watch includes the Music app. You can use it to control music playback on your iPhone, but it can also be used to play music directly from your Apple Watch.

Finding and Playing Music

You can launch the Music app from the Home screen. The Music app allows you to find music easily—it is sorted by artist name, album name, and song name.

1. Press the Digital Crown to show the Home screen.

2. Tap the Music app icon.

3. Tap Now Playing to see the current song playing and to control playback.

4. Tap Quick Play to start playing a random song in your collection.

5. Tap My Music to browse your music by artist, album, or song name.

6. Tap Playlists to use your pre-defined playlists of music.

7. Turn the Digital Crown to scroll up and select the source of your music. You can choose your iPhone or your Watch. There is more about how to load and play music on your Watch later in this chapter.

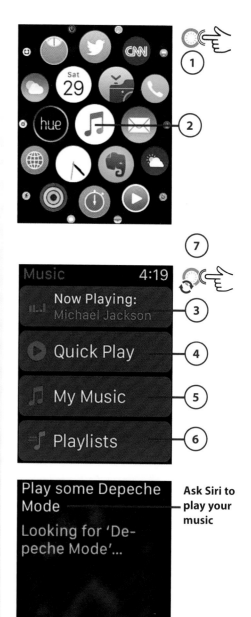

Tell Siri to Play Music for You

A very quick way to play the music you want is to activate Siri and ask her to play the music for you. For example, you can ask her to "play some Depeche Mode," and Siri searches your music collection for all songs by Depeche Mode and starts playing them for you. You can use variations of this by asking Siri to play a certain song by name, or even certain genres of music. For example, you can ask Siri to "play some dance music."

Ask Siri to play your music

My Music

The My Music screen allows you to quickly find and play music. You can choose to browse your music by artist, album, or song name. Follow steps 1-5 in the previous section to open the My Music screen.

1. Swipe left and right over the album cover art to scroll through your albums.

2. Tap an album cover to open that album.

3. Tap the down arrow to choose to see your music listed by artist, album, or song name.

4. Turn the Digital Crown to scroll up and down the list of artists, albums, or songs, whatever you have chosen to view in step 3.

Find Music by Artist

One of the ways to find a song you are looking for is to see the songs filtered by artist.

1. Tap the down arrow. If the selection already reads Artists, skip to step 3.

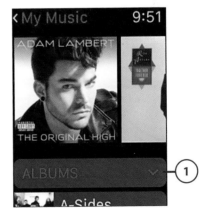

2. Tap Artists.

3. Turn the Digital Crown to scroll through the list of artists. If you scroll quickly, the scrolling mode switches to scrolling by first letter of the artist's name, allowing you to quickly find the artist's name.

4. Tap the name of the artist you want to hear.

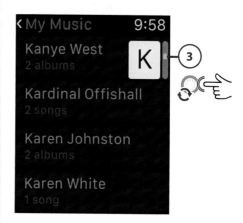

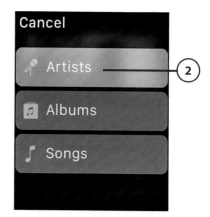

Tap to go back one screen

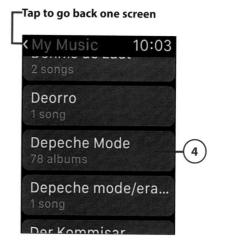

5. Turn the Digital Crown to scroll through the list of albums by the artist you have chosen.

6. Tap the album you want to hear.

7. Turn the Digital Crown to scroll through the list of songs on the albums.

8 Tap the play button to play the entire album in order starting from the first song.

9. Turn the Digital Crown to scroll through the list of songs on the albums.

10. Tap the song you want to hear.

Tap to go back one screen

Tap to go back one screen

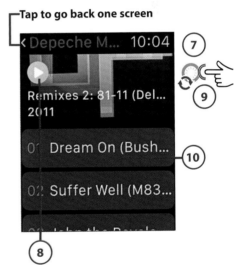

Find Music by Album

One of the ways to find a song you are looking for is to see the songs filtered by album.

1. Tap the down arrow. If the selection already reads Albums, skip to step 3.

2. Tap Albums.

3. Turn the Digital Crown to scroll through the list of albums. If you scroll quickly, the scrolling mode switches to scrolling by first letter of the album's name, allowing you to quickly find the album you are looking for.

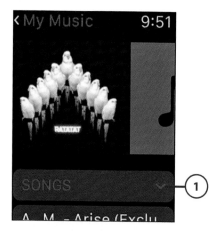

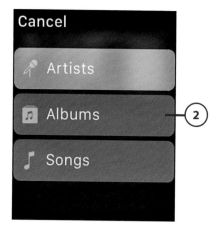

4. Tap the name of the album you want to hear.

5. Tap the play button to play the entire album in order starting from the first song.

6. Turn the Digital Crown to scroll through the list of songs on the albums.

7. Tap the song you want to hear.

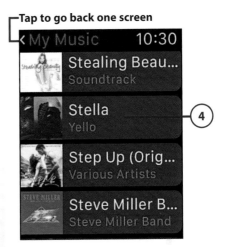

┌ **Tap to go back one screen**

┌ **Tap to go back one screen**

Find Music by Song Name

One of the ways to find a song you are looking for is to browse all the songs you have by song name.

1. Tap the down arrow. If the selection already reads Songs, skip to step 3.

2. Tap Songs.

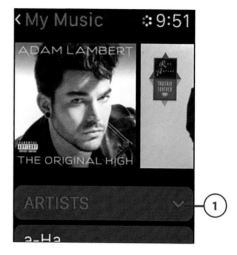

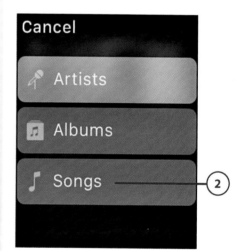

3. Turn the Digital Crown to scroll
   through the list of albums. If you
   scroll quickly, the scrolling mode
   switches to scrolling by first letter
   of the album's name, allowing you
   to quickly find the album you are
   looking for.

4. Tap the song you want to hear.

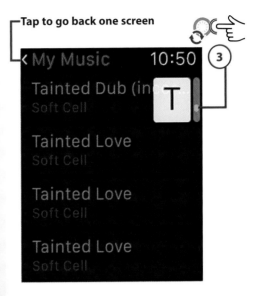

Tap to go back one screen

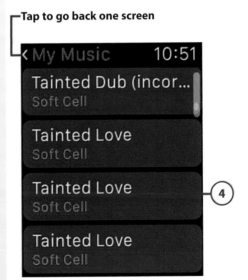

Tap to go back one screen

Find Music by Playlist

If you have one or more playlists on your iPhone that contain music grouped in custom ways, such as a playlist of songs to listen to during a workout and a playlist of songs to play at a party, you can play songs from those playlists or play the entire playlist using your Apple Watch.

1. Tap Playlists.

2. Turn the Digital Crown to scroll through the list of playlists.

3. Tap the playlist you want to see.

4. Tap the play icon to play the entire playlist starting from the first song.

5. Turn the Digital Crown to scroll through the list of playlists.

6. Tap the song you want to hear.

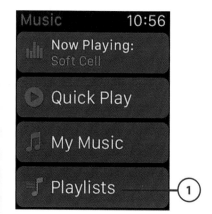

Controlling Playback

After you find the music you want to play, you can control the music playback on your iPhone using your Apple Watch, as well as access additional playback controls to play the music to other devices.

Use the Playback Controls to Play, Pause, and Jump to Other Songs

Whether you started playing music from a playlist, an album, or you started listening to Beats 1 on your iPhone, you can control the playback of the music using your Watch.

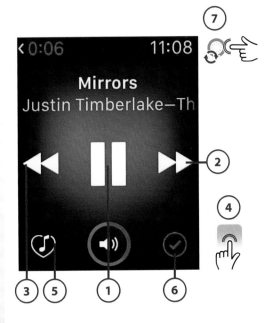

1. Tap the Pause button to pause playback. Tap again to resume playback.

2. Tap the Next Song icon to jump to the next song in the sequence.

3. Tap the Previous Song icon to jump to the previous song in the sequence.

4. Force Touch to see additional playback controls. We will cover these additional controls in the next section.

5. Tap the heart icon to indicate that you like the song that is playing. Apple uses this information to show you songs in the "For You" section in the Music app on your iPhone.

6. Tap the check icon to indicate that you would like this song removed from your music library.

7. Turn the Digital Crown to control the volume.

In What Sequence Are Songs Played Back?

The sequence depends on how you found the song in the first place. If you found it by browsing the list of artists or albums, when you tap to go to the next or previous song, the next or previous song on the album starts playing. If you tap to get to the next song and it's the last song on the album, playback stops. If the song is part of a playlist, then tapping to play the next or previous song plays the next or previous song in the playlist. If you found the song by searching the list of songs, then tapping the next or previous icon plays the next or previous song, respectively, in alphabetical order.

Use Additional Playback Controls to Repeat, Shuffle, and Play Music on Other Devices

During playback you can Force Touch on the screen to see additional controls, including repeating the song or all songs, shuffling your music, choosing an AirPlay device to play your music through, and choosing the source of your music.

1. Tap Repeat to choose whether you want to repeat the current song, repeat all songs, or turn repeat off.

2. Tap Shuffle to shuffle all songs so they play back in a random order, or choose to turn shuffle off.

3. Tap AirPlay to choose an AirPlay device on which you want to play the music. This can be any device that is Apple AirPlay compatible and is on the same network as your iPhone.

4. Tap Source to choose whether you want to play your music from your iPhone or Apple Watch. Certain conditions must be met to play music from your Watch, and those are covered in the next section.

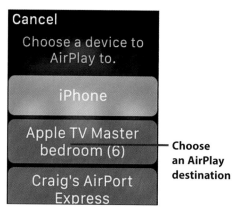

Choose an AirPlay destination

What Devices Support Apple AirPlay?

Devices can include an Apple Airport Express (if you have speakers attached to it), AirPlay-compatible speakers made by any manufacturer, an Apple TV, and any stereo receiver from any manufacturer that is Apple AirPlay compatible.

Playing Music from Your Apple Watch

Although you can use the Music app on your Apple Watch to control music playback on your iPhone, you can actually move a playlist of music to your Watch and play the music from your Watch without the need to have your iPhone with you. A typical use for this could be leaving your iPhone behind while you go for a run, and still being able to listen to your music from your Watch.

Creating a Playlist on Your iPhone

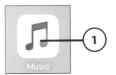

The first step in preparing to play music from your Watch is to create a playlist on your iPhone. If you already have a playlist created that you want to use, you can skip this section.

1. Tap the Music app icon on your iPhone.

2. Tap My Music.

3. Tap Playlists.

4. Tap New to create a new playlist.

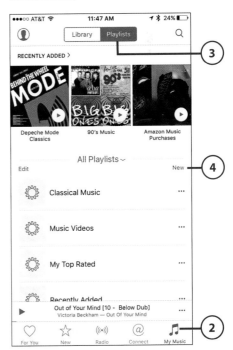

5. Type a name for your new playlist.

6. Tap Add Songs.

7. Tap the Search field and start searching for songs to add to your playlist.

8. Tap the plus symbol to the right of a song to add it to your playlist.

9. Tap Done when you have chosen all the songs you want in your playlist.

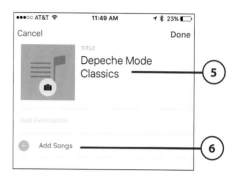

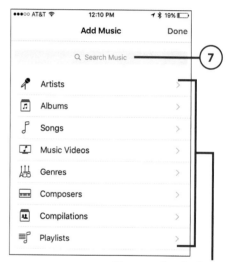

You can also find songs using these categories

Find more

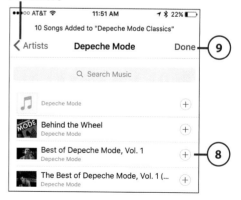

10. Tap Done to save your new
playlist.

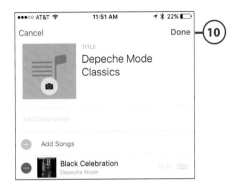

Synchronize a Playlist to Your Watch

Using the Apple Watch app on your
iPhone, you can choose one playlist
to synchronize to your Apple Watch.
Once synchronized, it is immediately
available for use.

1. Tap the Apple Watch app icon on
your iPhone.

2. Tap Music.

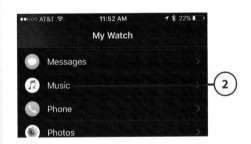

3. Tap Synced Playlist.

Defining Music Storage Limits

You can limit the amount of storage music uses on your Watch. To do this, tap Playlist Limit and then choose either a memory limit (such as 1GB) or a number of songs limit (such as 250 songs). When your chosen playlist is synchronized to your Watch, if there are more songs than the limit you set, the process synchronizes only up to the limit you set and then stops.

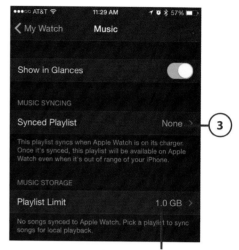

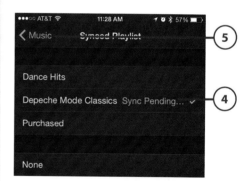

Choose how much space music will take on your Watch

4. Tap the playlist you want to synchronize to your Watch.

5. Tap Music to save your change and return to the previous screen.

6. Place your Watch on its charger, and wait for the playlist to synchronize. Once it completes, the percentage synced text changes to the name of the playlist.

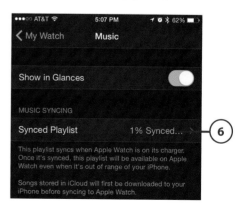

Pair a Bluetooth Device

Now that you have a playlist synchronized to your Watch, you need to pair a Bluetooth device to your Watch so that you have something to play the music through. Music cannot play through the speaker on your Watch. You need to purchase a Bluetooth headset or speaker before continuing.

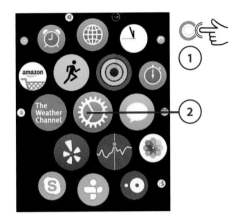

1. Press the Digital Crown to show the Home screen.

2. Tap the Settings icon.

3. Put your Bluetooth headset or speaker into pairing mode. The exact steps on how to do this differ by device manufacturer, so refer to the device's user guide.

4. Tap Bluetooth. Your Watch immediately starts searching for Bluetooth devices in range that are in pairing mode.

5. Tap your Bluetooth headset or speaker when you see it appear in the list of devices. In this example, a "JBL Flip 2" Bluetooth speaker is being paired.

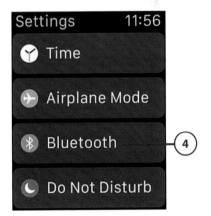

6. The status of your Bluetooth device changes from Not Paired to Connected, indicating that you have successfully paired it with your Watch.

Play a Playlist on Your Watch

Now that you have a playlist synchronized to your Watch, and a Bluetooth headset or speaker paired, you are ready to play songs in the playlist from your Watch.

1. From the Main Music app screen, use the Digital Crown to scroll up.

2. Tap Apple Watch.

Quickly Access Music Source

To quickly choose between your iPhone and Watch as the source of music, from anywhere in the Music app, Force Touch and tap Source.

3. Tap Playlists.

4. Notice that the Playlists screen now shows playlists on your Watch and on your iPhone. Tap the playlist you successfully synchronized to your Watch earlier.

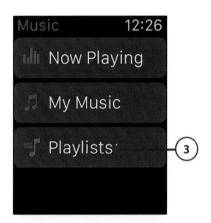

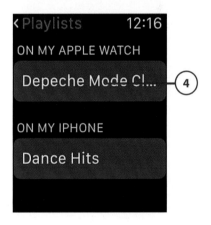

5. Tap the play icon to start playing the entire playlist, or tap a song, to start playing it from your Watch via the Bluetooth headset or speaker (not shown).

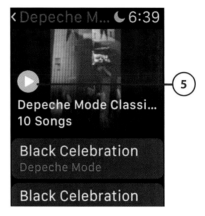

Using the Music Glance to Quickly Control Playback

The Music app has its own Glance, and you can use it to quickly control playback. To use it, raise your wrist and swipe up. Swipe left or right until you see the Music Glance. Using the Music Glance, you can pause and resume playing a song, move to the next or previous song, and adjust the volume using the Digital Crown.

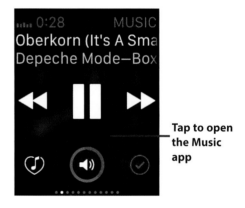

Tap to open the Music app

Paying using
your Watch

In this chapter, you learn how to use Apple Pay from your Watch. Topics include the following:

→ Using Apple Pay
→ Adding cards to Apple Pay

Using Apple Pay

You can use your Apple Watch to securely pay for items wirelessly, anywhere you see the Contactless Payment logo. Once you add a credit or debit card to your Watch, you are ready to go.

Adding Cards to Apple Pay

Before you start using Apple Pay on your Watch, you need to add one or more debit or credit cards. Even if you have previously added those same cards to Apple Pay on your iPhone, you need to add them to your Watch separately.

Don't I Need an iPhone 6 or iPhone 6 Plus to Use Apple Pay?

Before the Apple Watch arrived, you did need to have an iPhone 6 or iPhone 6 Plus or later to use Apple Pay. You can use your Apple Watch for Apple Pay now, so even if you own an older iPhone 5 or iPhone 5S, you can still use Apple Pay.

1. Tap the Apple Watch icon on your iPhone.

2. Tap Wallet & Apple Pay.

3. Tap Add Credit or Debit Card.

4. Tap Next.

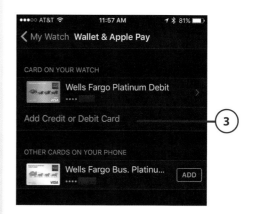

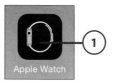

5. Position your debit or credit card in the frame. Your iPhone reads the relevant information off the card and continues automatically. If your iPhone is having trouble reading the information off your card, tap Enter Card Details Manually.

6. Check the information that your iPhone picked up from your card. Change it if it is incorrect.

7. Tap in the Security Code field to enter the security code from the back of your card.

8. Tap Next to continue. You might be prompted to agree to terms and conditions from your bank. If you are prompted, tap Agree to continue.

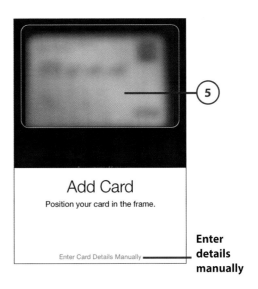

Add Card

Position your card in the frame.

Enter Card Details Manually

Enter details manually

●●●○○ AT&T 🔊   12:55 PM   ⚡ 🌀 ✳ 41% ⬛

❮ Back   Next

Card Details

Verify and complete your card information.

Name	CRAIG JOHNSTON
Card Number	
Expiration Date	
Security Code	Required

9. Choose a method by which you want to receive the verification code that finalizes the activation of your card in Apple Pay.

10. Tap Next.

11. Tap Verify when you receive the verification code from your bank via email or text message.

12. Tap Enter Code.

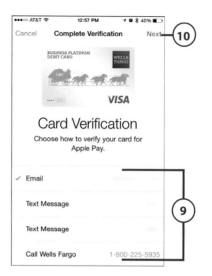

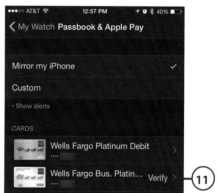

13. Enter the verification code you received from your bank.

14. Tap Next.

15. Tap Done.

16. You will receive an alert on your Watch notifying you that the card has been added successfully. Tap Dismiss. You are now ready to use Apple Pay from your Watch.

Pay with your Watch

Now that you have one or more cards added to Apple Pay on your Watch, you are ready to start securely paying wirelessly.

1. Before you use Apple Pay, make sure the payment terminal you are using supports Apple Pay. If you see the Contactless Payment logo, it means that the payment terminal includes a reader that supports Apple Pay.

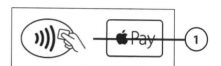

2. When you are ready to pay, double-press the Side Button on your Watch.

3. If you have more than one card added to Apple Pay and you want to switch cards, swipe left or right until you find the card you want to use.

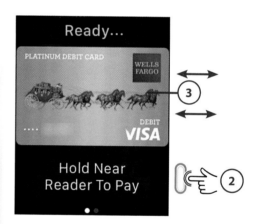

4. Hold the screen of your Watch near the payment terminal.

5. Once your card information has been read, you hear a tone from your Apple Watch and feel a tap on your wrist. A check mark also appears on the screen to confirm that you have paid.

>>>Go Further

WHAT IF I LOSE MY WATCH?

If you lose your Apple Watch, your credit cards are protected. When you set up Apple Pay on your Watch, you are required to choose a passcode, if you are not already using one. Once this passcode is entered, each time you take your Watch off, it locks itself. To unlock your Watch, you put it on your wrist and either type in the passcode or unlock your iPhone. This helps ensure that it is actually you wearing your Watch and using Apple Pay. If you lose your Watch, nobody else can use it for Apple Pay because they do not know your Watch passcode. You can also log in to iCloud and disable Apple Pay on your Watch, just in case. To do this, open http://iCloud.com in your desktop web browser, log in to your iCloud account, and click the Settings icon. Under My Devices, click your Apple Watch. Click Remove All to remove all debit and credit cards associated with Apple Pay on your Watch. This prevents anyone who happens to guess your Watch passcode from using Apple Pay.

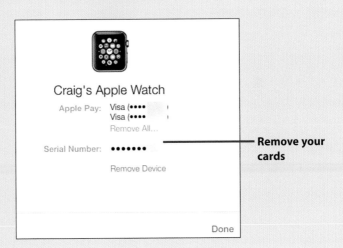

Remove your cards

Goal
achievements

In this chapter, you learn how your Watch keeps track of your activity and helps you stay healthy. Topics include the following:

→ Becoming familiar with the Activity app
→ Using the Workout app
→ Viewing detailed information in the Health app

Using Your Watch to Stay Active

Your Apple Watch automatically monitors your heart rate and activity to keep track of your health, and it allows you to record your workouts.

Becoming Familiar with the Activity App

The Activity app on your Watch keeps track of how often you stand up, how much you move around, and how much exercise you do.

1. Press the Digital Crown to see the Home Screen.

2. Tap the Activity app icon.

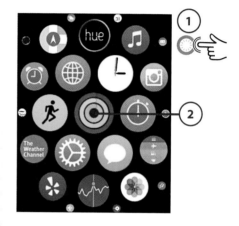

Navigate the Activity App on Your Watch

Using the Activity app on your Watch, you can view your activity information and change your Move Goal.

1. The Activity screen shows an overview of your activity. The blue ring shows how many times you have stood and moved around for 60 seconds or more, the green ring shows how much vigorous activity you have done so far, and the red ring shows you how much you have moved around.

2. Turn the Digital Crown to scroll down and see active calories, total number of steps, and total distance.

3. Swipe right to left through the screens to see your move progress.

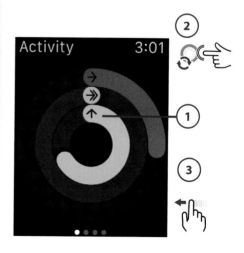

4. The Move screen shows you information specific to how many calories you have burned by moving so far.

5. Turn the Digital Crown to scroll down and see a graph showing calories burned per hour of the day.

6. Swipe left to see your exercise progress.

7. The Exercise screen shows you how many minutes of exercise you have done out of a total of 30 minutes. The Activity app records exercise as activities you do that are above and beyond your normal standing and walking around. It is loosely defined as an activity that is similar to a brisk walk.

Other Apps Count Toward Exercise

Third-party exercise apps, and the data they capture for your exercise, will count against the Exercise ring in the Activity app. This allows for a more complete picture of your exercise regardless of whether you use the Apple Workout app, or an exercise app from another software vendor.

8. Turn the Digital Crown to scroll down and see a graph showing exercise per hour of the day.

9. Swipe left to see your stand progress.

10. The Stand screen shows you how many hours of the day you stood up and walked around, up to a maximum of 12 hours. Within each hour, if you stood up and walked around for at least 60 seconds, you are credited with standing during that hour.

11. Turn the Digital Crown to scroll down and see a graph showing each of the 12 hours and which ones you stood up during.

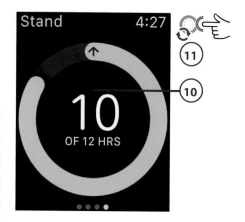

Change Your Move Goal

If you want to change your Move Goal (that is, how many calories you want to try to burn during a single day), do the following:

1. Force Touch on any screen of the Activity app.

2. Tap to change Move Goal.

3. Turn the Digital Crown to adjust the number of active calories you want to aim to burn each day. Tap Update to make the change.

Time to Stand Up

If you haven't stood up and moved around for at least 60 seconds during a given hour of the day, 10 minutes before the top of that hour, the Activity app prompts you to stand up.

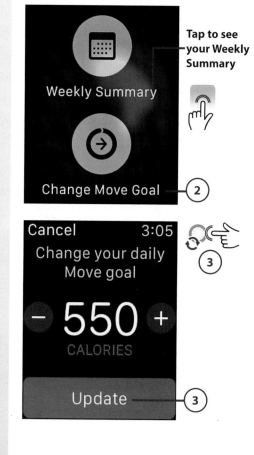

Tap to see your Weekly Summary

Use the Activity App on your iPhone

Using the Activity app on your iPhone, you can view your activity information per day in more detail, including seeing active and resting calories, number of minutes of exercise, how often you stood, and information about workouts.

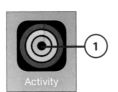

1. Tap the Activity app icon on your iPhone.

2. Tap the Today icon to show today's activity.

3. Tap a specific day in the week to show activity for that day.

4. Swipe left or right over the days of the week to show previous or next weeks.

5. Tap the month to show your activity overview for.

6. Swipe up to see more detailed move, exercise, and stand information.

7. Swipe left across the Move graph to see active, resting, and total calories burned.

8. Swipe left across the Exercise graph to see how many minutes you exercised and the total time you were active.

9. Swipe up to see the stand information.

Your activity overview

10. Swipe right to left across the Stand graph to see how many hours you were idle as well as how many hours went by when you stood up.

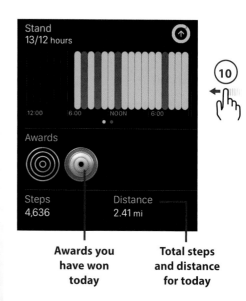

See Workout Information

If you worked out on the day you are viewing in the Activity app on your iPhone, you can scroll down to the bottom of the list of information to see your workout summary. Tap the right arrow to see the full information about your workout.

Awards you have won today

Total steps and distance for today

Using the Workout App

When you work out, you can use the Workout app to keep track of your heart rate, activity, number of minutes you worked out, and calories burned.

1. Press the Digital Crown to see the Home Screen.

2. Tap the Workout app icon.

Start a Workout with Siri

You can ask Siri to start a workout. To do this, activate Siri and tell her to "start a workout." Siri launches the Workout app for you. You can also use Siri for a more complete workout command like "start a 20 minute outdoor walk."

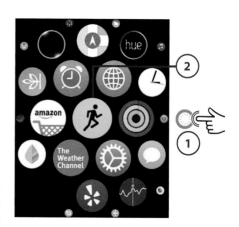

Choose a Type of Workout and Start Your Workout

After the Workout app starts, you can choose the type of workout you are about to do as well as select the type of goal you want to set for the workout.

1. Turn the Digital Crown to scroll up and down the list of workout types.

2. Tap the type of workout. For this example, use the Outdoor Walk workout.

3. Swipe left and right to choose what goal you want to set yourself for the workout. You can choose an active calorie burn goal, a time goal, or a distance goal, or you can choose OPEN for no goal.

4. Turn the Digital Crown to adjust the value on the goal you have chosen.

5. Tap Start to start your workout.

6. Wait for the countdown to reach zero and then start your workout.

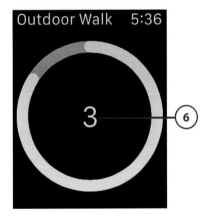

View Information and End Your Workout

While you work out, you can see activity-related information in real time on your Watch. When you finish your workout, you can save the record of your workout.

1. Lift your wrist to see information relevant to your workout.

2. Swipe left and right to see all the information, including your real-time heart rate. Depending on the type of workout you have chosen, the information shown includes elapsed time, pace, distance, and active calories burned.

3. Force Touch the Watch screen when you have finished your workout and then tap End.

4. Turn the Digital Crown to scroll through the summary of your workout.

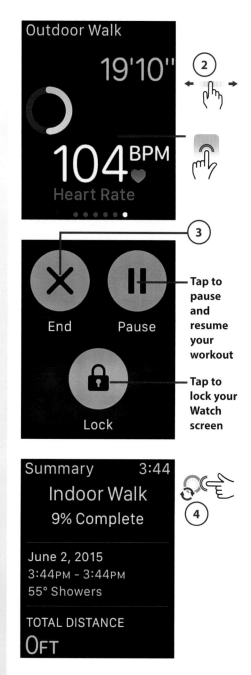

Tap to pause and resume your workout

Tap to lock your Watch screen

5. Tap Save to save the record of your workout.

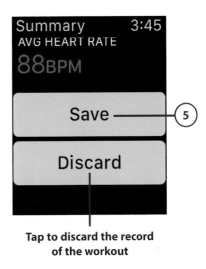

Tap to discard the record of the workout

Using the Health App

The Health app on your iPhone is the central hub for all your health data. This includes the data collected by your Apple Watch, but it also includes data collected by other health-related apps on your iPhone as well as other types of medical hardware such as scales and blood pressure monitors. Using the Health app gives you a much deeper understanding of your health, and helps you take steps to become healthier.

1. Tap the Health app icon.

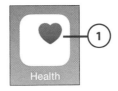

2. Swipe down to see more of your Dashboard.

3. Tap Health Data to see granular information about the health data being gathered and shared with the Health app.

4. Tap Sources to choose which devices and apps share their health data with the Health app, and which apps can read health data from the Health app.

5. Tap Medical ID to create or edit your medical ID.

6. Tap Day, Week, Month, or Year to adjust the range for the Dashboard.

Rearrange the Dashboard

To rearrange the Dashboard, touch and hold on a section and move it up and down to reposition it. Tap a section to see more information about that section's health data.

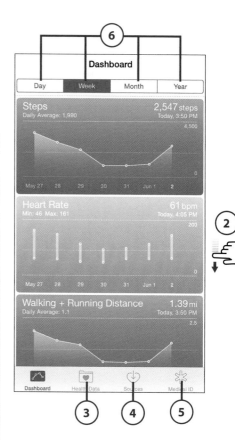

Choose Health Sources

You can choose to allow other apps on your iPhone to read information gathered by the Health app. Then, you can decide which apps and devices can report information to the Health app.

1. Tap Sources.

2. Tap the name of an app to choose what data it can share with the Health app as well as what data it can read from the Health app. In this example, we will choose the Lose It! app.

3. Choose what data the app collects to share with the Health app.

4. Swipe down to choose what data the app can read from the Health app.

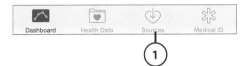

5. Choose what data the Health app collects from other sources to share with the app.

6. Tap Sources to save your changes and return to the previous screen.

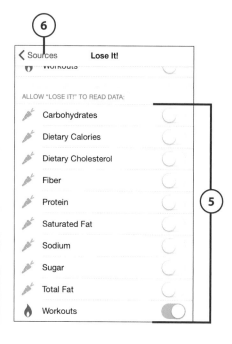

> >>>*Go Further*
>
> ## CLARIFYING SOURCES
>
> In the example used for the preceding task, the Lose It! app is shown. You can use it to track your food intake by using your iPhone's camera to scan the barcodes on the food you eat, and the Lose It! app automatically tracks the information about that food. For this example, the Lose It! app is configured to share all the information it collects with the Health app. Also, the Lose It! app is configured to only read Workout data from the Health app. You don't need it to collect the other data, because the Lose It! app is the one already gathering that data and sharing it with the Health app. The process is the same for all apps and devices you use—for example, sleep analysis bands, Wi-Fi scales, and blood pressure bands.

View the Health Data

Your Apple Watch, along with your iPhone, other health and fitness apps, and other medical devices such as Wi-Fi scales, sleep analysis bands, and blood pressure bands, all report their data to the Health app. Here is how to drill down into that data.

1. Tap Health Data.

2. Tap a data category. In this example, Fitness is used in order to look at the data collected by the Apple Watch.

3. Tap the type of data you want to see. In this example, notice the workout data that the Apple Watch has been tracking and submitting to the Health app.

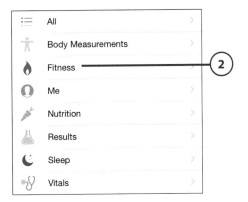

4. Show on Dashboard lets you choose whether you want to have this health data on your Dashboard.

5. Tap Add Data Point if you want to manually add a data point (in this case, a workout) that is missing from the collected data for some reason.

6. Tap Share Data to choose what apps to share this data with and to see what apps or devices provided this data.

7. Tap Show All Data to see all apps or devices that provided this data and drill into each data point.

8. Tap a data point to see all the information about it.

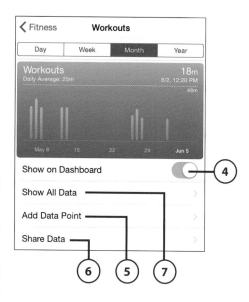

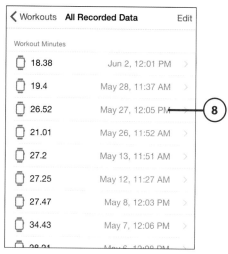

9. Tap Back once you are finished looking at the information.

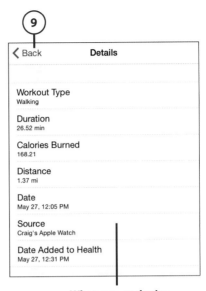

What app or device provided the information

App installing —

In this chapter, you learn how to find apps for your Watch, install them, and manage them. Topics include the following:

→ Finding Watch apps
→ Installing and removing Watch apps
→ Managing Watch apps

Installing and Managing Watch Apps

Many of the iPhone apps you already use might include Apple Watch apps that extend the functionality of the app to your Watch. Regular iPhone apps that include an Apple Watch app have that additional app bundled in with the regular iPhone app. If you have an Apple Watch, the Watch app can be installed on your Watch. If not, the Watch app just stays dormant inside the iPhone app.

Finding Watch Apps

You might already have apps on your iPhone that include a Watch app, but you can also find more Watch apps using the iTunes App Store on your iPhone.

1. Tap the Apple Watch app icon on your iPhone.

2. Tap Featured to see featured Apple Watch apps.

3. Tap Categories to browse for Watch apps by category.

4. Swipe up to scroll down the page and see all featured apps.

5. Tap an app to see more information about the app as well as screenshots of the app running on a Watch and iPhone.

Tap to search for Watch apps

Installing Watch Apps

When you install a Watch app, you are really installing an iPhone app that contains a Watch app within itself, and that Watch app then installs on your Watch.

1. Tap the app that you want to install.

2. Swipe up to scroll down the page to see the screenshots of the app running on a Watch and iPhone.

3. Tap the price of the app to buy it. If the app is free, you will see a button labeled GET.

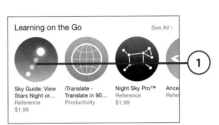

What Happens After the App Installs?

After the app installs on your iPhone, a few seconds later the app installs on your Watch. If you look at the Home Screen on your Watch, you can see the app installing.

App installing on your Watch

Managing Your Watch Apps

You can manage which apps you want to install on your Watch, rearrange the Home Screen layout, decide if Watch apps should automatically install, and choose which apps can notify you on your Watch.

Choose Watch Apps to Install or Uninstall

At any time you can decide to install or uninstall a Watch app. The Watch app remains part of the iPhone app, ready to be installed on your Watch, unless you remove the iPhone app.

1. Tap the Apple Watch app icon on your iPhone.

2. Tap the name of the app that you want to install or uninstall.

3. Tap the Show App on Apple Watch On/Off switch to install or uninstall the Watch app. If the switch is on, the app has been installed, and switching it off uninstalls the app.

4. Tap the Show in Glances On/Off switch to show the app's Glance view in Glances. Not all Watch apps have a Glance view, so this option might not be available.

5. Tap My Watch to return to the previous screen.

Rearrange App Icons

When you install a new Watch app, that app's icon appears on the Home Screen in a random position. You can rearrange your Home Screen to move app icons to a more appropriate place.

1. Tap the Apple Watch app icon on your iPhone.

2. Tap App Layout.

3. Touch and hold on an app icon that you want to reposition. The app icon becomes larger.

4. Drag the app icon to its new position and then lift your finger to release it. The new arrangement appears on your Apple Watch.

5. Tap My Watch to return to the previous screen.

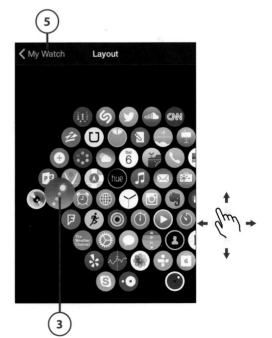

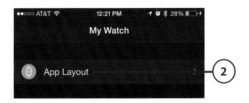

Decide Whether Apps Should Automatically Install

By default, when you install an iPhone app that contains a Watch app (or you update an existing iPhone app, and the updated app contains a Watch app), the Watch app will automatically install on your Watch. You can control this behavior.

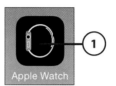

1. Tap the Apple Watch app icon on your iPhone.

2. Tap General.

3. Tap App Install.

4. Tap the Automatic App Install On/Off switch to choose whether Watch apps are automatically installed on your Watch when an iPhone app with a Watch app is installed on your iPhone.

5. Tap General to return to the previous screen.

Change App Notification Settings

When an app runs on your Watch, by default it is set to mirror the notification settings that are set for that same app on your iPhone. You can override that setting and silence alerts from specific apps.

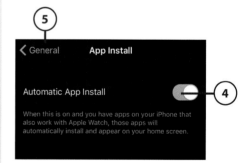

1. Tap the Apple Watch app icon on your iPhone.

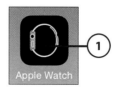

2. Tap Notifications.

3. Tap the On/Off switch next to an app to choose whether you want the app alerts to be mirrored on your Watch.

4. Tap My Watch to return to the previous screen.

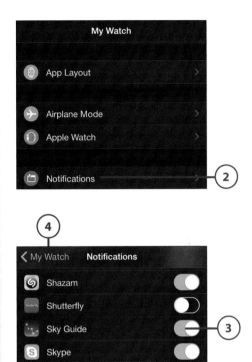

>>>Go Further
HOW MUCH MEMORY ARE MY APPS USING?

To see how much memory (storage) each Watch app is using, open the Apple Watch app on your iPhone. Tap General and then tap Usage. After a few seconds you can see how much memory each app is using, sorted by the apps with the most memory usage on top. You also see the total amount of memory being used, and how much is available. Because you have a limited amount of memory set aside for Watch apps, you can use this screen to decide which apps to uninstall to make room for a new app that you want to install.

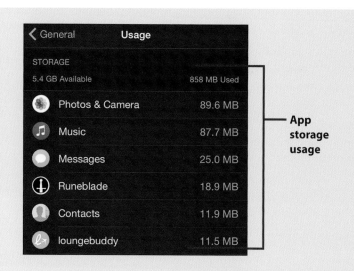

Control your
Apple TV or Mac
from your Watch

In this chapter, we cover other useful Watch apps not yet covered in this book. Topics include the following:

→ Control your Apple TV
→ Control your iPhone camera
→ Compose and send a tweet

9

Using Other Watch Apps

There are many other apps on your Watch that we have not yet covered. This chapter covers some of the most useful Watch apps. If you see an app discussed in this chapter, but you don't have it on your Watch, install it from the iTunes App Store. Chapter 8, "Installing and Managing Watch Apps," provides more information on how to install Watch apps.

Using Media-Related Apps

You can control your Apple TV or Mac from your Watch, as well as control playback on third-party music apps such as Pandora, and even control your iPhone's camera.

Control Your Apple TV or Mac

The Remote app on your iPhone and Watch allows you to control your Apple TV or iTunes running on your Mac. All the devices you want to control must be using the same Apple ID.

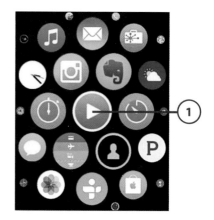

1. Tap the Remote app icon. You can also tell Siri to "start remote."

2. Turn the Digital Crown to scroll through the list of available Apple TVs and Macs to control.

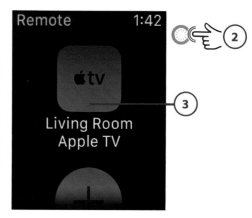

3. Tap the Apple TV or Mac that you want to control. In this example, an Apple TV is chosen.

4. Swipe up, down, left, or right to move the cursor or selection box on your Apple TV. This is equivalent to pressing the up, down, left, or right button on the Apple TV's physical remote control.

5. Tap Menu to go back one screen on your Apple TV. This is equivalent to pressing the Menu button on the Apple TV's physical remote control.

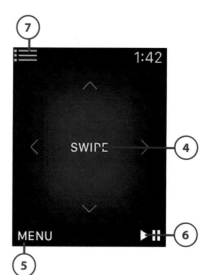

6. Tap the Play/Pause icon to play, resume playing, or pause audio or video on your Apple TV. This is equivalent to pressing the Play/Pause button on the Apple TV's physical remote control.

7. Tap the List icon to see a list of other devices you can control.

>>>Go Further
CONTROLLING YOUR MAC

If you select a Mac to control, you are actually controlling iTunes on the Mac. Instead of the Apple TV remote view, you see a music playback screen, allowing you to play or pause music as well as jump forward or backward through a playlist or album. You can control the volume by turning the Digital Crown. If you Force Touch the screen, you can choose an AirPlay device to play the music through.

Music controls

>>>Go Further
ADD A NEW DEVICE TO CONNECT TO

As you might have done on your iPhone before, you add new Apple TVs and Macs to control from the Remote app on your Watch by pairing them. To do this, when you see the list of available devices, if you turn the Digital Crown to scroll down to the bottom of the list, you see a plus symbol. If you tap the plus symbol, you can add a new Apple TV or Mac to control. You are presented with a number on the screen. The number on the screen needs to be typed into the Apple TV or Mac you want to control to complete the pairing.

Control Pandora

If you use Pandora on your iPhone, you can control it using the Pandora app on your Watch. The Pandora app on your iPhone must already be configured with your Pandora username and password.

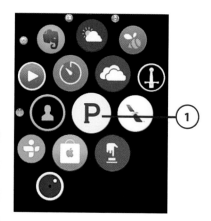

1. Tap the Pandora app icon. You can also tell Siri to "start Pandora."

2. Turn the Digital Crown to scroll through the list of stations and recommended stations.

3. Swipe left to control playback.

4. Tap the pause icon to pause and resume playing the music.

5. Tap the thumbs down icon to indicate that you do not like the song that is currently playing.

6. Tap the thumbs up icon to indicate that you like the song that is currently playing.

7. Tap the jump forward icon to jump to the next song.

8. Swipe left to control the volume.

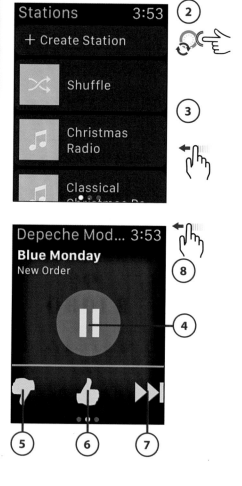

9. Tap the plus icon to increase the volume.

10. Tap the minus icon to decrease the volume.

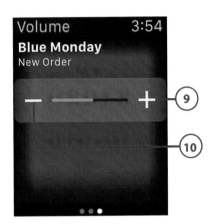

Control Your iPhone's Camera

You can use your Watch as a remote control for your iPhone's camera. This allows you to place your iPhone somewhere but still take pictures, and even set a timer. A common use for this would be taking a group shot with you in the frame.

1. Tap the Camera app icon. Even if your iPhone is asleep and locked, the Camera app launches. You can also ask Siri to "take a picture."

2. Tap to set focus and exposure on the area of the picture you have tapped.

3. Tap the Timer icon to set a timer for 3 seconds and take a burst of 10 pictures automatically.

4. Tap the Shutter icon to take a picture. If you hold the shutter icon, you take multiple pictures in a burst mode.

5. Tap the thumbnail of the pictures you have taken to view them full screen.

6. Press the Digital Crown to exit the Camera app remote control. The Camera app on your iPhone will also close.

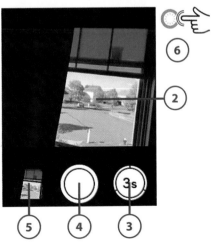

DO OTHER CAMERA APPS HAVE WATCH APPS?

Other camera apps that you have installed to use in addition to the built-in iPhone camera app do have their own remote controls. The only difference between the built-in Camera app and these third-party camera apps is that the Watch app does not have the ability to launch a third-party camera app for you on your iPhone; you will need to manually launch it. Once it's launched, the Watch app for that camera app is able to remotely control it.

Using Social Media Apps

Not all social media apps have Watch apps. As of the writing of this book, Facebook, for example, has no Watch app, but others such as Twitter and Instagram do, thus allowing you view and respond to posts or tweets.

Using Instagram

The Instagram Watch app allows you to view your feed and see your own activity. When viewing a post, you can "like" it and make a quick comment using emojis.

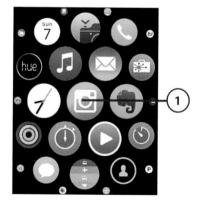

1. Tap the Instagram app icon. You can also tell Siri to "start Instagram."

Acting on Instagram Posts

While viewing a post on Instagram, including your own posts, you can tap the heart icon to "like" the photo, or you can tap the More icon (three horizontal dots) to read all of the comments as well as post your own comment using emoji.

2. Tap Feed to see your Instagram feed.

3. Tap Activity to see your Instagram activity.

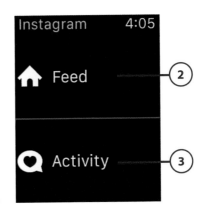

Using Twitter

The Twitter Watch app allows you to see your own timeline as well as the top trending topics and their associated tweets. You can also use Siri to post your own tweet.

1. Tap the Twitter app icon. You can also tell Siri to "start Twitter."

2. Tap Timeline to see your Twitter timeline.

3. Tap Top Trends to see the top trending Twitter topics.

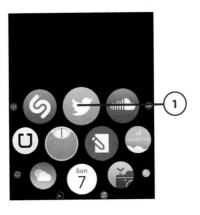

Acting on Tweets and Tweeting from Your Watch

While viewing a tweet, you can reply to the tweet, retweet it, or mark it as a favorite tweet. If you Force Touch on the screen, you can compose your own tweet. You can either share your location, tweet only emoji, or dictate your tweet using Siri.

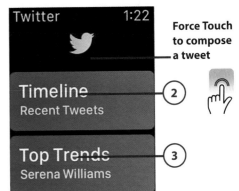

Force Touch to compose a tweet

Using Time- and Date-Related Apps

You can look at your calendar, set a timer, start a stopwatch, set an alarm, and see the time from around the world.

Start a Timer

Being able to quickly start a timer can be very useful for many activities, including preparing food and making drinks. You can ask Siri to start a timer, or you can do it manually.

1. Tap the Timer app icon.

2. Turn the Digital Crown to set the amount of time the timer should run for.

3. Tap Start to start the timer.

4. Tap Reset to reset the timer.

Start a Timer Using Siri

A far more efficient way to start a timer is to use Siri. To do this, raise your wrist and say, "Hey Siri," and then tell Siri how long you want the timer set for. For example, you can say "set a timer for 15 minutes." Siri starts the Timer app, sets the timer, and automatically starts the countdown.

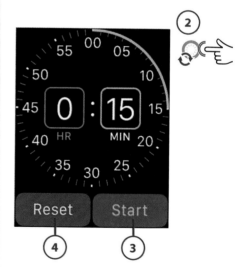

Use the Stopwatch

Your Watch includes a stopwatch with lap time functionality. You can change the stopwatch display using a Force Touch.

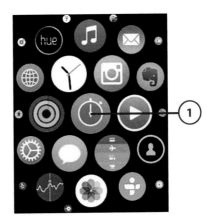

1. Tap the Stopwatch app icon. You can also ask Siri to "start a stopwatch."

2. Tap the start/stop icon to start or stop the stopwatch.

3. Tap the lap icon to start the lap counter.

4. Force Touch to choose the type of display used by the stopwatch. You can choose between analog, digital, graph, and a hybrid display.

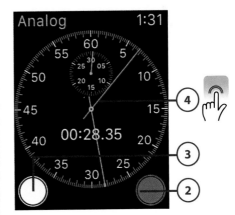

See the Time Around the World

Your Watch includes a World Clock app that can be used to see the time in different cities around the world. The exact cities it shows time for must be set up using the Clock app on your iPhone.

1. Tap the World Clock app icon.

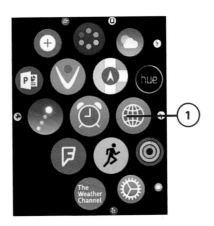

2. Turn the Digital Crown to scroll through all the cities you previously set up.

3. Tap a city to see the time in that city.

4. Tap World Clock to return to the list of cities.

Ask Siri the Time in Any City

Regardless of which cities you have set up in the World Clock app, you can always ask Siri to tell you the time in any city in the world. To do this, raise your wrist and say, "Hey Siri." Then, ask her for the time in a particular city. For example, you can ask her, "What's the time in Cape Town?"

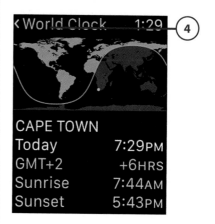

Managing Alarms

The Alarm Clock app on your Watch allows you to create and remove alarms as well as edit them. Alarms can be set to repeat every day or only certain days.

1. Tap the Alarm Clock app icon. A list of current alarms will be shown. You can also ask Siri to "open alarms."

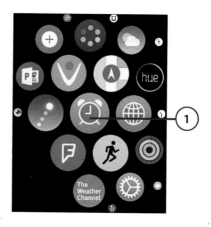

2. Tap the On/Off switch to turn on or off an alarm.

3. Tap an alarm to edit or delete it.

4. Force Touch to create a new alarm.

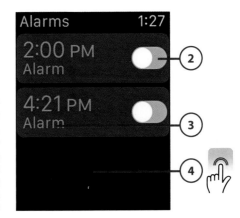

>>>Go Further

ASK SIRI TO SET YOUR ALARMS

Instead of manually setting your alarms using the Alarm Clock app, you can ask Siri to manage your alarms. To do this, first activate Siri by raising your wrist and saying "Hey Siri." Then, give Siri an alarm command. For example, you can tell Siri to "wake me up every weekday at 7 a.m." and she creates a new alarm for 7 a.m. that recurs only on weekdays. You could also tell Siri to "set an alarm for 4 hours from now" or "set an alarm for 4 a.m."

It's Not All Good

Alarms Not Synchronized

One oddity of setting alarms on your Watch is that, unlike other apps, alarms do not synchronize back to your iPhone. So when you set an alarm on your Watch, if you happen to look at the alarms you have set in the Clock app on your iPhone, you will not see it there and will not be able to manage it.

See the Weather Around the World

Your Watch includes a Weather app that can be used to see the weather in different cities around the world. The exact cities it shows the weather for must be set up using the Weather app on your iPhone.

1. Tap the Weather app icon.

2. Swipe left and right to scroll through the cities where you have chosen to keep track of the weather. The leftmost city is always the city you are currently in.

3. Turn the Digital Crown to scroll down to the 10-day forecast for the selected city.

4. Force Touch to change the display to show hourly conditions, percentage rain, or temperature.

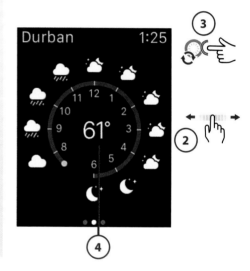

>>>Go Further

ASK SIRI THE WEATHER IN ANY CITY

Regardless of which cities you have set up in the Weather app, you can always ask Siri to tell you the weather in any city in the world. To do this, raise your wrist and say, "Hey Siri." Then, ask for the weather in a particular city. For example, you can ask, "What's the weather in Cape Town?" You can also be creative and ask, "Will it be snowing in Wellington, New Zealand tomorrow?" or "Will I need an umbrella next week in New York?"

Check on Your Schedule

The Calendar app on your Watch allows you to see your meetings, get directions to an address shown in the meeting, or call the meeting participants.

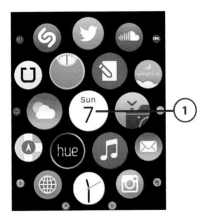

1. Tap the Calendar app icon.

2. Turn the Digital Crown to scroll through the hours of the day.

3. Tap an event to see information about it.

4. Force Touch to switch between Day and List views. The Day view shows events for today only, whereas the List view shows all events in chronological date order.

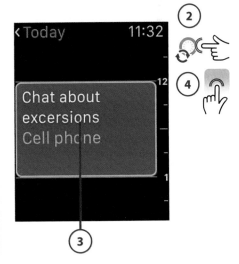

>>>Go Further

ASK SIRI TO MANAGE YOUR CALENDAR

The Calendar app itself has limited functionality; however, using Siri you can create new calendar events, change events, and remove events. To do this, activate Siri by raising your wrist and saying, "Hey, Siri." Next, tell Siri what you want her to do. For example, you can say "schedule a meeting with Karen tomorrow at 2 p.m." or "change my 3 p.m. meeting to 3:30 p.m." or even "cancel my 4 p.m. meeting."

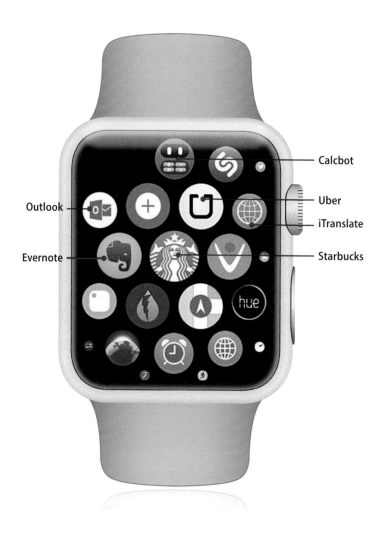

Calcbot

Outlook

Uber

iTranslate

Evernote

Starbucks

In this chapter, you learn about useful Watch apps that you might want to try. Topics include the following:

→ Travel related apps, including Uber and iTranslate
→ Working with Evernote, Outlook, and PowerPoint

10

Useful Watch Apps

There are many Watch apps made by companies that already make iPhone apps. Their Watch apps normally complement their iPhone apps, or extend functionality to your Watch. If you see an app discussed below, but you don't have it on your Watch, install it from the iTunes App Store. Chapter 8, "Installing and Managing Watch Apps," provides more information on how to install Watch apps.

Calling an Uber Car

Apps on your iPhone that keep you informed or help you get from one place to another when traveling are very useful. Having those apps on your Apple Watch is even more convenient. Companies such as Uber have Watch apps that allow you to call a car, and most airlines have Watch apps that allow you to keep up to date on your flight details. This task details getting a ride from Uber. Remember, this app does not come preinstalled; you need to download it to your iPhone and Watch from the App Store.

1. Tap the Uber app icon. You can also tell Siri to launch Uber.

2. Tap Request after the Uber app determines your location and length of time for a car to arrive.

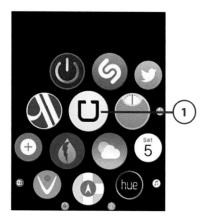

3. Turn the Digital Crown to scroll down to see your driver and car information.

4. Tap Dismiss to see the progress of the driver to your location.

5. Force Touch to cancel your car request.

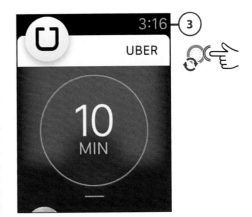

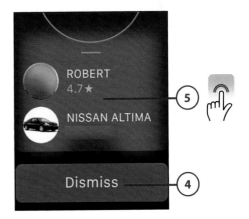

Calculating the Tip Using Calcbot

Calcbot is a full-fledged calculator app, but it also allows you to do conversions, for example between miles and kilometers, or between currencies. The Watch app has a handy feature to calculate tips and handle split bills when dining out.

1. Tap the Calcbot app icon. You can also tell Siri to launch Calcbot.

2. Tap Tip Calc.

3. Enter the total amount of the bill.

4. Turn the Digital Crown to scroll down and select the tip percentage and how many people are paying.

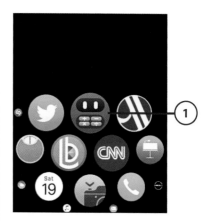

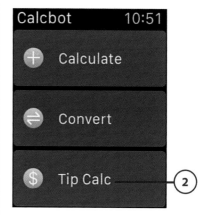

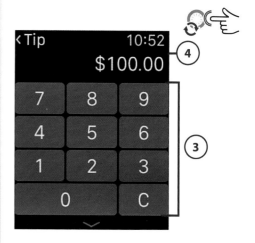

5. Tap the minus and plus icons to decrease or increase the percentage of the tip.

6. Tap the minus and plus icons to decrease or increase how many people are paying for the check/bill. The amount owed by each person is shown at the bottom.

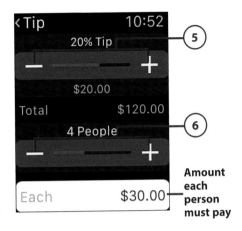

Amount each person must pay

Finding a Starbucks and Checking Your Rewards

If you have a Starbucks gift card, or just want to find a Starbucks close by, you can use the Starbucks app on your Watch. To pay for Starbucks using your Starbucks gift card, the card must be added to the Wallet app on your iPhone.

1. Tap the Starbucks app icon. You can also ask Siri to launch Starbucks.

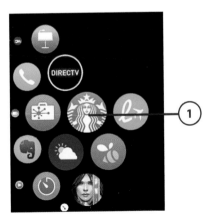

2. See your Starbucks reward level on the first screen.

3. Tap Rewards to see and use any Starbucks rewards you have.

4. Swipe to the left to see Starbucks nearby.

5. Force Touch to choose between seeing any Starbucks nearby, Starbucks nearby that have a drive through lane, and Starbucks nearby that let you reserve your coffee ahead of time.

6. Turn the Digital Crown to scroll down and see the selected Starbuck's amenities.

7. Tap a green icon to open Apple Maps on your Watch and get directions to the selected Starbucks location.

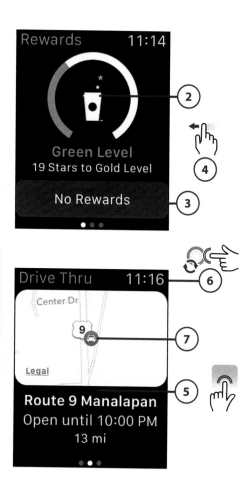

Translating Your Words

If you have the iTranslate app, you can use it on your Watch to speak a phrase and have the translation appear onscreen and even have the translation spoken. This is very useful if you are traveling in a foreign country and you need to communicate with someone who does not speak your language.

1. Tap the iTranslate app icon.
   You can also ask Siri to launch
   iTranslate.

2. Force Touch if you need to change
   the language. If not, skip to step 6.

3. Tap Change Language.

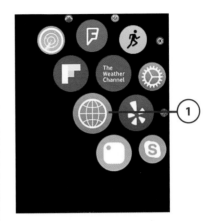

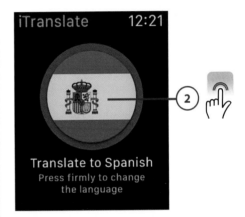

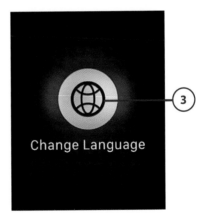

4. Use the Digital Crown to scroll through the list of available languages.

5. Tap the language you want to translate your word into.

6. Tap the flag to start speaking.

7. Start speaking when you see the wave form at the bottom of the screen.

8. Tap Done when you are finished speaking.

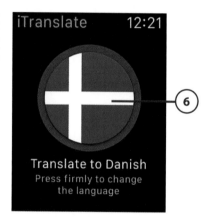

9. The translation will appear on the screen. Show your Watch to the person you are speaking with, so they can read the translated text.

10. Tap the speaker icon if you would rather let your Watch speak the translation.

11. Adjust the volume using the Digital Crown.

12. Tap Done return to the main iTranslate screen.

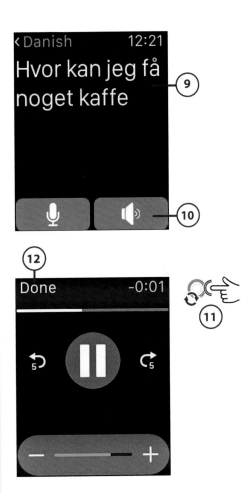

Working with Email Using Outlook

If you use Microsoft Outlook on your iPhone to connect to your work email (or your personal email on Outlook.com), you can use the new Outlook Watch app to read and reply to your email.

Read Email As It Arrives

You can read and act on an email as it arrives in your Outlook Inbox, and you are notified on your Watch.

1. Raise your wrist when you feel the notification tap.

2. Turn the Digital Crown to scroll through the email and see actions you can take on it.

3. Tap Archive to send the email to the Archive folder.

4. Tap Delete to delete the email and move it to the Trash folder.

5. Tap Schedule to have this email reappear at some time in the future. After tapping Schedule, choose the time to have the message reappear.

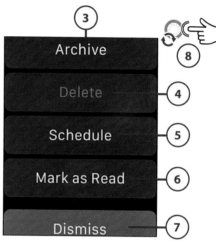

Not Scheduling?

As of the time of this writing, this feature was not yet working. When it does begin working, the process should appear as noted in step 5.

---

6. Tap Mark as Read to mark the email as read.

7. Tap Dismiss to leave the email as unread.

8. Turn the Digital Crown to scroll back up to the text of the email.

9. Tap the email to reply to it. Your Watch opens the Outlook app and displays the Inbox. Follow from step 2 in the next section titled "Read Emails From the Outlook App" for instructions on replying to an email.

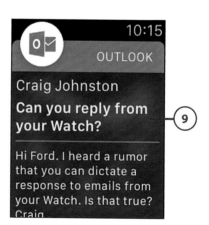

Read Emails From the Outlook App

You can also read and act on any email message at any time by opening the Outlook app on your Watch.

1. Tap the Outlook app icon. You can also ask Siri to launch Outlook.

2. Tap the email you want to read and reply to.

3. Turn the Digital Crown to scroll through the email and see actions you can take on the email.

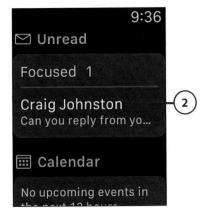

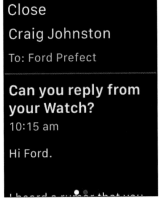

4. Tap to the flag the email.

5. Tap Schedule to have this email reappear at some time in the future.

Move to the Next Email

If you would rather leave this email and act on the next email in your Inbox, swipe left.

6. Tap the Reply or Reply All icons to reply to the sender of the email, or reply to the sender and all recipients in the Carbon Copy (CC) field.

7. Tap to reply using one of the Quick Replies. Scroll through the Quick Replies using the Digital Crown.

8. Tap to reply to the email using Emoji.

9. Tap to dictate a reply to the email.

10. When you see the wave form at the bottom of the screen, speak your response.

11. Tap Done when you have finished speaking and your reply is sent.

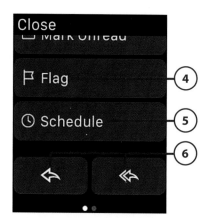

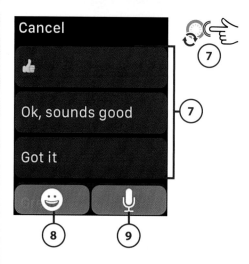

>>>Go Further

ACTING ON MEETING INVITES

If you receive an invitation to a meeting, you can respond to it on your Watch. This works whether you see the invite in a notification as it arrives, or later if you open the Outlook app. If you see a meeting invitation arrive as a notification, use the Digital Crown to scroll down and choose whether you want to Accept the meeting, Maybe Accept the meeting (this is the same as Tentatively accepting), Decline the meeting, or dismiss the notification and respond to the invitation later. If you open the Outlook app and you see a pending meeting invite, tap to open it. Use the Digital Crown to scroll down to choose whether you want to Accept the meeting, Accept Tentatively, or Decline the meeting.

Using Evernote

Evernote is a popular organization tool that allows you to write and organize notes. The Evernote Watch app allows you to find and view notes and dictate new notes.

1. Tap the Evernote app icon. You can also tell Siri to launch Evernote.

2. Turn the Digital Crown to see more recently updated notes.

3. Tap a recently updated note to open it.

4. Tap to search for a note.

5. Tap to dictate a new note.

6. When you see the wave form appear at the bottom of the screen, start speaking.

7. Tap Done when you have finished dictating your note.

8. Tap to save your new note.

Be Reminded with a Note

In Evernote, when you dictate a new note, before saving it, you can tap the clock icon to set a time when you want to be reminded of the note. Some of your reminder choices include: This Afternoon, Tomorrow, and Next Week. Tap the reminder option you want, and then tap Save to save the note.

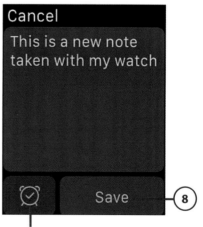

Set a note reminder

Controlling Your PowerPoint Presentation

If you use your iPhone to present Microsoft PowerPoint presentations via AirPlay or by directly connecting your iPhone to the projector with a VGA cable, you can use your Watch to control the presentation. Before using the PowerPoint Watch app, you must already have a presentation open in the PowerPoint app on your iPhone.

1. Tap the PowerPoint app icon. You can also tell Siri to launch PowerPoint.

2. Tap to start the presentation.

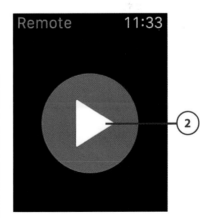

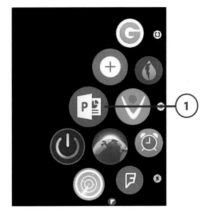

3. Tap the arrows to navigate forward and backward through the slides.

4. Force Touch to restart or end your presentation.

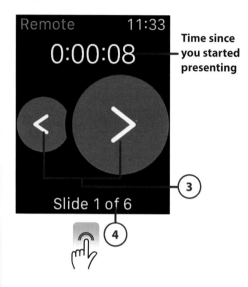

Time since you started presenting

Index

Symbols

24-Hour Time On/Off switch (Clock app), 86

A

About option (General Settings), 66

accepting meeting invitations, 247

Accessibility settings, 69-71

Achievements On/Off switch (Activity app), 84

actions
   Digital Crown, 15-16
   Side Button, 17

activating
   Apple Pay, 17

Siri, 137-138
   by pressing Digital Crown, 138
   by raising wrist, 138

Activity app
   first-time setup, 13
   on iPhone, 199-200
   launching, 196
   Move Goal, 198
   navigating, 196-198
   personal information, 82
   settings, 82-84

Add Credit or Debit Card option (Apple Pay), 188

Add Data Point option (Health app), 208

Add Songs option (Music app), 178

Add to Favorites option (Maps app), 152

adjusting. *See* personalization; settings

Airplane mode, 58-61

AirPlay devices, 176-177

AirPlay option (Music app), 176

Alarm Clock app, 230-231

alarms

editing, 231

managing with Siri, 139-140

removing, 231

setting, 230-231

synchronization, 231

albums

music albums, 170-171

photo albums, synchronizing, 41-45

Albums option (Music app), 170

animations, limiting, 70

answering calls, 128-129

app icons, moving, 52-53

App Layout, 52-53

App Layout option, 215

Apple ID, 67

Apple Maps. *See* Maps app

Apple Pay

activating, 17

adding cards to, 187-191

disabling, 193

making purchases with, 192

removing cards from, 193

requirements, 187

security, 193

settings, 95-96

Apple TV, controlling from Watch, 222-223

Apple Watch app, 6

Apple Watch updates, 27

apps, 211

Activity app

first-time setup, 13

on iPhone, 199-200

launching, 196

Move Goal, 198

navigating, 196-198

personal information, 82

settings, 82-84

Alarm Clock, 230-231

app icons, moving, 52-53

Apple Pay, 95-96

Apple Watch, 6

automatic download, 216

Calcbot, 237-239

Calendar, 85-86, 233

Camera, 225-226

Clock, 86-87

Contacts

placing calls from, 132-133

settings, 88

Evernote, 247-248

finding, 212

Friends

placing calls from, 135

settings, 89-90

Health

choosing health sources, 205-206

launching, 203-204

navigating, 203-204

viewing health data, 207-209

Instagram, 226-227

installing

automatically, 216

choosing apps to install, 214

manually, 213

iTranslate, 240-243

launching with Siri, 146

Lose It!, 206

Mail, 90-91, 126-128

Maps, 149

actions while navigating, 153

directions, 151-157

landmark information, 158

launching, 150

locations, 150-155

Maps Glance, 150

navigation taps, 153

settings, 92

memory usage, 217-218

Messages. *See* Messages

Music, 165

accessing music source, 182

creating playlists, 177-179

finding music by album, 170-171

finding music by artist, 167-169

finding music by playlist, 174

finding music by song name, 172-173

launching, 166

Music Glance, 184

My Music screen, 167

navigating, 166

pairing Bluetooth devices, 181-182

playback controls, 175-177

playing playlists, 182-184

sequence of playback, 176

settings, 94-95

synchronizing playlists, 179-180

notification settings, 216-217

Outlook, 245-247

Pandora, 224-225

Phone, 96-97, 130

Photos

creating Photo watch faces, 47-48

settings, 98

synchronizing photo albums, 41-45

PowerPoint, 249-250

rearranging app icons, 215

Remote, 222-223

running, 24

Siri. *See* Siri

Starbucks, 239-240

Stocks, 99

Stopwatch, 229

third-party Watch app settings, 102-103

Timer, 228

Twitter, 227

Uber, 236-237

uninstalling, 214

Wallet, 95

Weather, 100, 232

Workout, 200-203

ending workouts, 202-203

launching, 200

settings, 101

starting workouts, 201

viewing workout information, 202-203

World Clock, 229-230

archiving email, 127, 244

artists, finding music by, 167-175

Artists option (Music app), 168

Ask Before Deleting option (Mail app), 91

asking Siri

calendar questions, 145

math questions, 146

sports-related questions, 143-144

stock questions, 145

time-related questions, 143, 230

weather questions, 144, 232

audio. *See* sound

Audio Messages option (Messages app), 93

Automatic Downloads, 67, 216

Automatically Download Apps On/Off switch, 216

automatically installing Watch apps, 216

B

back of Watch

heart rate sensor, 6

microphone, 5

speaker, 5

Watch band release buttons, 5

Bluetooth devices

pairing, 181-182

settings, 181-182

Bold Text, 70, 73

brightness settings, 72-73

C

Calcbot app, 237-239

calculating tips with Calcbot, 237-239

Calendar, 233

accessing with Siri, 145

events, creating, 142

checking, 233

managing, 233

settings, 85-86

calling Uber cars, 236-237

calls, 128

ending, 130

favorites, 131

handling incoming calls, 128-129

managing recent calls, 131

muting, 130

Phone app, 130

placing

from Contacts, 132-133

from email, 126

from Friends app, 135

voicemail, 133-134

volume controls, 130

Camera app, 225-226

canceling

alarms, 140

reminders, 141

timers, 141

cards

adding to Wallet, 95

removing from Apple Pay, 193

cars (Uber), calling, 236-237

Categories (iTunes App Store), 212

Change Move Goal option (Activity app), 198

changing. *See* personalization; settings

checking

    memory usage for Watch apps, 217-218

    schedule, 233

choosing

    health sources, 205-206

    Photo Album watch face, 45-46

    Watch apps to install/uninstall, 214

    watch faces, 30-31

City Abbreviations option (Clock app), 87

clearing notifications, 22

Clock app, 86-87

clock apps

    Alarm Clock, 230-231

    Clock, 86-87

    Stopwatch, 229

    Timer, 228

    World Clock, 229-230

color of emojis, changing, 109

commands. *See* questions (Siri)

complications, 20, 34

composing messages

    from Friends list, 115

    from Messages app, 112-114

configuration. *See* settings

connecting devices, 223

Contactless Payment logo, 192

Contacts app

    getting directions to contacts, 156-157

    placing calls from, 132-133

    settings, 88

controlling

    music playback

        Music Glance, 184

        playback controls, 175-177

    PowerPoint presentations, 249-250

coordinating Airplane mode, 58-61

Create Message option (Messages app), 114

Create Watch Face option (Photos app), 48

creating

    alarms, 139

    calendar events, 142

    Glances, 63-65

    Photo watch face, 47-48

    playlists, 177-179

    reminders, 140-141

    timers, 141

    watch faces, 36-38

credit cards

    adding to Apple Pay, 187-191

    adding to Wallet, 95

    removing from Apple Pay, 193

current location, displaying, 150

Customize button, 32

customization. *See* personalization

D

Dashboard (Health app), 204

date- and time-related apps. *See also* Calendar

    Alarm Clock, 230-231

    Clock, 86-87

    Stopwatch, 229

Timer, 228

World Clock, 229-230

Day view (Calendar), 233

debit cards

adding to Apple Pay, 187-191

adding to Wallet, 95

removing from Apple Pay, 193

declining meeting invitations, 247

Default Card option (Apple Pay), 96

Default City option (Weather app), 100

Default Replies (Mail app), 90

Default Replies option (Messages app), 93

Default Stock option (Stocks app), 99

deleting. *See* removing

devices, connecting, 223

Diagnostics, 9

dictating

email, 123

Maps app, 151

messages, 107

Digital Crown

actions, 15-16

explained, 4

pressing to activate Siri, 138

Digital Touch, 117

receiving, 120-121

replaying, 121

sending, 118-120

directions

getting, 151-153

actions while navigating, 153

to contacts, 156-157

to locations, 151-153

to pinned locations, 155

handing off between iPhone and Watch, 154

disabling Apple Pay, 193

dismissing

email, 244

messages, 106

displaying

Apple ID, 67

current location, 150

Friends list, 17, 25

Glances, 146

health data, 207-209

landmark information, 158

sender details (messages), 111

timers, 141

workout information, 202-203

Display Order (Contacts app), 88

Do Not Disturb mode, 53-57

double-tapping, 18

dragging, 18

driving directions. *See* directions

E

editing. *See also* personalization; settings

alarms, 231

calendar events, 142

email

archiving, 127, 244

deleting, 127, 244

dismissing, 244

handing off to iPhone or Mac, 125

Mail app, 126-128

marking

　as read, 244

　as unread, 127

multiple email notifications, 124

reading, 121-122

　from notifications, 244

　from Outlook Watch app, 245-247

replying to

　dictation, 123

　emojis, 124

　from within notifications, 122

scheduling, 244-246

emojis

adding to email, 124

adding to messages, 108-109

ending

phone calls, 130

workouts, 202-203

Enter Card Details Manually option (Apple Pay), 189

Enter Code option (Apple Pay), 190

Evernote app, 247-248

exercise apps. See also Health app

Activity, 196-200

　on iPhone, 199-200

　launching, 196

　Move Goal, 198

　navigating, 196-198

Workout, 200-203

　ending workouts, 202-203

　launching, 200

　starting workouts, 201

　viewing workout information, 202-203

Exercise screen (Activity app), 197

external features, 3

Digital Crown, 4, 15-16

heart rate sensor, 6

microphone, 5

Side Button, 5, 17

speaker, 5

touchscreen, 4, 18

Watch band release buttons, 5

F

faces. See watch faces

favorites

adding, 131

calling, 131

Maps app, 152

featured apps, 212

Featured option (iTunes App Store), 212

finding

music

　by album, 170-171

　by artist, 167-169

　by playlist, 174

　by song name, 172-173

Starbucks locations, 239-240

Watch apps, 212

first-time setup, 6-14

Activity app, 13

Bluetooth pairing, 7

Diagnostics, 9

language, 6

left/right wrist setting, 7

Location Services, 8

passcodes, 10

Siri, 9

synchronization, 12

terms and conditions, 8

Watch apps, 11-13

fitness apps. *See also* Health app

Activity, 196-200

first-time setup, 13

on iPhone, 199-200

launching, 196

Move Goal, 198

navigating, 196-198

personal information, 82

settings, 82-84

Workout, 200-203

ending workouts, 202-203

launching, 200

starting workouts, 201

viewing workout information,
202-203

Flag Style option (Mail app), 91

Force Touch, 18

Friends app

placing calls from, 135

settings, 89-103

Friends list, 25

composing messages from, 115

viewing, 17, 25

front of Watch

Digital Crown, 4, 15-16

Side Button, 5, 17

touchscreen, 4, 18

G

General Settings, 65

Accessibility, 69-71

changing, 66-69

Software Update, 27

gestures

Digital Crown, 15-16

Side Button, 17

touchscreen, 18

getting directions

actions while navigating, 153

to contacts, 156-157

to locations, 151-153

to pinned locations, 155

Glances

adding, 63-65

Music Glance, 184

overview, 23, 61

rearranging, 61-63

scrolling through, 61

viewing with Siri, 146

Goal Completions On/Off switch
(Activity app), 83

Grayscale setting, 70

H

handing off, 68

directions, 154

email, 125

incoming calls, 128-129

messages, 116-117

Siri, 146-147

Handoff, 146-147

directions, 154

email, 125

explained

incoming calls, 128-129

messages, 116-117

Siri, 146-147

haptics settings, 73-75

Messages app, 93

Phone app, 97

Health app

choosing health sources, 205-206

launching, 203-204

navigating, 203-204

viewing health data, 207-209

health data, viewing, 207-209

Health Data option (Health app), 204, 207

health-related apps

Activity, 196-200

launching, 196

Move Goal, changing, 198

navigating, 196-198

on iPhone, 199-200

Health, 203-209

choosing health sources, 205-206

launching, 203-204

navigating, 203-204

viewing health data, 207-209

Workout, 200-203

ending workouts, 202-203

launching, 200

starting workouts, 201

viewing workout information, 202-203

health sources, choosing, 205-206

heart rate sensor, 6

heartbeat

heart rate sensor, 6

receiving, 120

sending, 118

I-K

iCloud, Apple Pay settings, 193

icons

moving, 52-53

rearranging, 215

iMac

controlling from Watch, 222-223

handing off to

email, 125

messages, 116-117

iMessages. *See Messages*

Include Mail option (Mail app), 90

informational Siri requests

calendar requests, 145

math questions, 146

sports-related questions, 143-144

stock questions, 145

weather questions, 144

Instagram Watch app, 226-227

installing Watch apps

automatically, 216

choosing apps to install, 214

manually, 213

interacting with Apple Watch

complications, 20

Digital Crown, 15-16

Friends list, 25

Glances, 23

Lock screen, 19

notifications, 21-22

running apps, 24

Side Button, 17

Siri, 26

touchscreen, 18

invitations (meeting), responding to, 247

Invitations option (Calendar app), 85

Invitee Responses option (Calendar app), 85

iPhone

Airplane mode, 58-61

Camera, controlling from Watch, 225-226

Handoff

directions, 154

email, 125

explained, 68

messages, 116-117

Siri, 146-147

pairing with Apple Watch, 7

synchronizing with Apple Watch, 12

taking calls on, 129

iTranslate app, 240-243

iTunes App Store, 212

L

landmark information, viewing, 158

Language & Region settings, 67

languages

settings, 6, 67

translating, 240-243

launching apps

Activity app, 196

Health app, 203-204

Maps app, 150

Music app, 166

with Siri, 146

Workout app, 200

left/right wrist setting, 7

List view (Calendar), 233

Location Services, 8

locations

adding to favorites, 152

current location, displaying, 150

landmark information, 158

pinning on map, 155

sending your location, 111

Starbucks locations, finding, 239-240

Lock screen, 19

Lose It! app, 206

lost Watches, 193

M

Mac

controlling from Watch, 222-223

handing off to

email, 125

messages, 116-117

Mail app, 90-91, 126-128

making phone calls

from Contacts app, 132-133

from email, 126

from Friends app, 135

managing

alarms, 139-140

calendar, 233

recent calls, 131

reminders, 140-141

Watch apps

automatic download, 216

choosing apps to install/uninstall, 214

Maps app, 149

actions while navigating, 153

directions

to contacts, 156-157

handing off between iPhone and Watch, 154

to locations, 151-153

to pinned locations, 155

landmark information, 158

launching, 150

locations

adding to favorites, 152

current location, displaying, 150

pinning on map, 155

searching for, 151-153

Maps Glance, 150

navigation taps, 153

settings, 92

Maps Glance, 150

marking email

as read, 244

as unread, 127

math-related Siri requests, 146

media-related apps, 221

Pandora, 224-225

Remote app, 222-223

Medical ID option (Health app), 204

meeting invitations, responding to, 247

memory usage (apps), 217-218

Menu option (Remote app), 222

Message Preview option (Mail app), 90

Messages, 105

composing

from Friends list, 115

new messages, 112-114

dismissing, 106

handing off, 116-117

reading

from Messages app, 110-111

from notifications, 106

responding to

default replies, 106

dictation, 107

emojis, 108-109

from Messages app, 110-111

sending your location, 111

sender details, viewing, 111

settings, 92-93

microphone, 5

mirroring Airplane mode, 58-61

Mirror My iPhone option

Apple Pay, 95

Calendar app, 85

Contacts app, 88

Mail app, 90

Messages app, 92

Phone app, 97

Photos app, 98

missed notifications, 21

MMS (Multimedia Message Service) messages. *See* Messages

Mono Audio setting, 71

Monogram option (Clock app), 87

monuments, viewing information about, 158

Motion & Fitness privacy settings, 80-82

Move Goal, 198

Move screen (Activity app), 197

moving app icons, 52-53

Multimedia Message Service (MMS) messages. *See Messages*

multiple email notifications, 124

museums, viewing information about, 158

Music app, 165

    accessing music source, 182

    Bluetooth devices, pairing, 181-182

    finding music

        by album, 170-171

        by artist, 167-169

        by playlist, 174

        by song name, 172-173

    launching, 166

    Music Glance, 184

    My Music screen, 167

    navigating, 166

    playback controls, 175-177

    playlists

        creating, 177-179

        playing, 182-184

        synchronizing to Watch, 179-180

    sequence of playback, 176

    settings, 94-95

Music Glance, 184

muting audio, 130

My Music option (Music app), 166

N

navigating

    Activity app, 196-198

    Health app, 203-204

    Music app, 166

    My Music screen, 167

navigation taps (Maps app), 153

Next Song icon (Music app), 175

notes

    creating reminders from, 248

    taking with Evernote, 247-248

notifications

    app notification settings, 216-217

    clearing, 22

    listening to voicemail from, 134

    missed notifications, 21

    overview, 21-22

    privacy, 77

    reading email from, 244

    reading messages from, 106

    replying to email from, 122

    settings, 76-77

Notifications Indicator On/Off switch (Clock app), 87

Now Playing option (Music app), 166

O

On/Off Labels setting, 70

Organize By Thread option (Mail app), 91

Outdoor Walk workout (Workout app), 201

Outlook Watch app, 245-247

P

Pace View (Workout app), 101

pairing Bluetooth devices, 181-182

Pandora app, 224-225

parks, viewing information about, 158

Passbook. *See* Wallet

passcodes, 193

  first-time setup, 10

  how it works, 10

  passcode-related settings, 78-79

Pause button (Music app), 175

pausing timers, 141

payments, making with Apple Pay, 192

personalization

  Airplane mode, 58-61

  app icons, moving, 52-53

  app settings

    Activity app, 82-84

    Apple Pay, 95-96

    Calendar app, 85-86

    Clock app, 86-101

    Contacts app, 88

    Friends app, 89-101

    Mail app, 90-91

    Maps app, 92

    Messages app, 92-93

    Music app, 94-95

    Passbook, 95

    Phone app, 96-97

    Photos app, 98

    Stocks app, 99

    Weather app, 100

    Workout app, 101

  brightness, 72-73

color of emojis, 109

Do Not Disturb, 53-103

General Settings, 65

  Accessibility, 69-71

  changing, 66-69

  Software Update, 27

Glances

  adding, 63-65

  overview, 61

  rearranging, 61-103

  scrolling, 61

haptics settings, 73-75

Motion & Fitness privacy settings, 80-82

Move Goal, 198

notifications settings, 76-77

passcode-relate settings, 78-79

sound settings, 73-75

text size, 72-73

watch faces, 29-36

  changing watch face functionality, 49-51

  choosing, 30-31

  creating new version of existing watch face, 36-38

  customizing, 31-36

  deleting, 38-40

  displaying time ahead of actual time, 50

  Photo Album watch face, 40-48

  Photo watch face, 40-48

Phone app, 96-97, 130

phone calls

  calling favorites, 131

  ending, 130

  handling incoming calls, 128-129

  managing recent calls, 131

muting, 130

Phone app, 96-97, 130

placing

   from Contacts, 132-133

   from email, 126

   from Friends app, 135

voicemail, 133-134

volume controls, 130

Photo Album watch face

   choosing, 45-46

   overview, 40

   synchronizing photo albums, 41-45

photo albums, synchronizing, 41-45

Photo watch face

   creating, 47-48

   overview, 40

   synchronizing photo albums, 41-45

Photos app

   creating Photo watch faces, 47-48

   settings, 98

   synchronizing photo albums, 41-45

Photos Limit option, 44, 98

phrases, translating, 240-243

pinning locations on map, 155

places

   adding to favorites, 152

   current location, displaying, 150

   landmark information, 158

   pinning on map, 155

placing phone calls

   from Contacts, 132-133

   from email, 126

   from Friends app, 135

playing

   music

      controlling playback, 175-177

      creating playlists, 177-179

      Music Glance, 184

      pairing Bluetooth devices, 181-182

      playing playlists, 182-184

      sequence of songs, 176

      Siri, 166

      synchronizing playlists, 179-180

   voicemail, 133-134

Playlist Limit option, 180

Playlist option (Music app), 177

playlists

   creating, 177-179

   finding music by, 174

   playing, 182-184

   synchronizing to Watch, 179-180

Playlists option (Music app), 166, 174, 183

Play/Pause icon (Remote app), 222

powering off Apple Watch, 17

PowerPoint presentations, controlling, 249-250

PowerPoint Watch app, 249-250

Power Reserve mode, 17

Power Saving Mode (Workout app), 101

presentations (PowerPoint), controlling, 249-250

Previous Song icon (Music app), 175

privacy settings

   Motion & Fitness, 80-82

   notifications, 77

Progress Updates option (Activity app), 83

Push Alerts from iPhone On/Off switch (Clock app), 86

Q

questions (Siri)
  calendar questions, 145
  math questions, 146
  sports-related questions, 143-144
  stock questions, 145
  time-related questions, 143, 230
  weather questions, 144, 232
quick messages, 106
Quick Play option (Music app), 166
Quick Replies (email), 246

R

raising wrist to activate Siri, 138
reading
  email, 121-122
    from notifications, 244
    from Outlook Watch app, 245-247
  messages
    from Messages app, 110-111
    from notifications, 106
rearranging
  app icons, 215
  Glances, 61-63
  Health Dashboard, 204
receiving Digital Touch, 120-121
recent calls, managing, 131
Reduce Motion setting, 70
Reduce Transparency setting, 70

reminders
  canceling, 141
  creating from notes, 248
  setting, 140-141
Remote app, 222-223
remote control
  Apple TV, 222-223
  Camera, 225-226
  Macs, 222-223
  Pandora, 224-225
Remove Pin option (Maps app), 155
removing
  alarms, 231
  email, 127, 244
  map pins, 155
  Maps favorites, 152
  watch faces, 38-40
Repeat Alerts option (Messages app), 93
Repeat option (Music app), 176
replaying
  Digital Touch, 121
  voicemail, 134
replying
  to email
    dictation, 123
    emojis, 124
    from notifications, 122, 244
    from Outlook Watch app, 245-247
  to meeting invitations, 247
  to messages
    default replies, 106
    dictation, 107
    emojis, 108-109
    from Messages app, 110-111
    sending your location, 111

requests (Siri). *See* questions (Siri)

Reset option (General Settings), 68

resetting timer, 228

responding

to email

dictation, 123

emojis, 124

from notifications, 122, 244

from Outlook Watch app, 245-247

to meeting invitations, 247

to messages

default replies, 106

dictation, 107

emojis, 108-109

from Messages app, 110-111

sending your location, 111

retweeting tweets, 227

right/left wrist setting, 7

running Watch apps, 24

S

schedule, checking, 233

scheduling email, 244-246

screen brightness, 72-73

scrolling Glances, 61

Search field (Music app), 178

searching

for music

by artist, 167-175

by playlist, 174

for places, 151-153

security

Apple Pay, 193

motion and fitness privacy settings, 80-82

passcodes, 78-79, 193

Security Code field (Apple Pay), 189

Send Location option, 111

Send Read Receipts option (Messages app), 93

sending

Digital Touch, 118-120

email

dictation, 123

emojis, 124

from within notifications, 122, 244

messages

default replies, 106

dictated responses, 107

emojis, 108-109

from Friends list, 115

from Messages app, 112-114

your location, 111

setting

alarms, 139-140, 230-231

reminders, 140-141

timers, 141

settings

Activity app, 82-84

app notifications, 216-217

Apple Pay, 95-96, 193

Bluetooth, 181-182

Brightness & Text Size, 72-73

Calendar app, 85-86

Clock app, 86-87

Contacts app, 88

Do Not Disturb, 53-57

Friends app, 89-90

General Settings, 65

   Accessibility settings, 69-71

   changing, 66-69

   Software Update, 27

haptics, 73-75

Mail app, 90-91

Maps app, 92

Messages app, 92-93

Motion & Fitness privacy settings, 80-82

Music app, 94-95

Notifications, 76-77

passcode-related settings, 78-79

Phone app, 96-97

Photos app, 98

sound, 73-75

Stocks app, 99

third-party Watch apps, 102-103

Time, 50-51

Wallet, 95

Weather app, 100

Workout app, 101

setting up Apple Watch, 6-14

   Activity app, 13

   Bluetooth pairing, 7

   Diagnostics, 9

   language, 6

   left/right wrist setting, 7

   Location Services, 8

   passcodes, 10

   Siri, 9

   synchronization, 12

   terms and conditions, 8

   Watch apps, 11-13

Share Data option (Health app), 208

Shared Calendar Alerts option (Calendar app), 85

Short Message Service (SMS) messages. *See* Messages

Short Name option (Contacts app), 88

Show Alerts option

   Calendar app, 85

   Mail app, 90

   Messages app, 93

   Phone app, 97

   Photos app, 98

Show All Data option (Health app), 208

Show App on Apple Watch option, 103, 214

Show Goal Metric option (Workout app), 101

Show in Glances option, 214

   Maps app, 92

   Music app, 94

   Stocks app, 99

   third-party apps, 103

showing. *See* displaying

Shuffle option (Music app), 176

Side Button, 5, 17

Signature (Mail app), 91

Siri, 26

   activating, 137-138

      by pressing Digital Crown, 138

      by raising wrist, 138

   alarms

      canceling, 140

      setting, 139, 231

calendar
creating events, 142
editing events, 142
managing, 233
first-time setup, 9
Glances, viewing, 146
handing off to your iPhone, 146-147
launching apps with, 146
math questions, 146
music, playing, 166
reminders
canceling, 141
setting, 140-141
sports-related questions, 143-144
stock questions, 145
time-related questions, 143, 230
timers
canceling, 141
pausing, 141
setting, 141
starting, 228
weather questions, 144, 232
workouts, starting, 200
size of text, 72-73
sketches
receiving, 120
sending, 119-120
smiley icons. See emojis
SMS (Short Message Service) messages. See Messages
social media apps
Instagram, 226-227
Twitter, 227
Software Update, 27, 67
song name, finding music by, 172-173

Songs option (Music app), 172
Sort Order (Contacts app), 88
sound
Messages app, 93
Mono Audio setting, 71
muting, 130
Phone app, 97
settings, 73-75
Source option (Music app), 176, 182
Sources option (Health app), 204-205
speaker, 5
speech recognition. See Siri
sports-related information, finding, 143-144
Stand screen (Activity app), 198
Starbucks app, 239-240
Start option (Maps app), 152
Start Pairing command, 7
starting
stopwatch, 229
timer, 228
workouts
manually, 201
with Siri, 200
stock information, asking Siri for, 145
Stocks app, 99
Stopwatch app, 229
storage limits (music), 180
swiping, 18
Synced Album option, 43, 98
Synced Playlist option, 94, 180
synchronizing
alarms, 231
iPhone with Apple Watch, 12
photo albums, 41-45
playlists, 179-180

T

taking notes with Evernote, 247-248

tapping, 18

terms and conditions, 8

text messages. *See* Messages

text size, 72-73

time

    displaying time ahead of actual time, 50-51

    Time Travel feature, 51

Time Lapse watch face, 48

time-related apps

    Alarm Clock, 230-231

    Clock, 86-87

    Stopwatch, 229

    Timer, 141, 228

    World Clock, 229-230

time-related Siri requests, 139

    alarms, 139-140

        canceling, 140

        creating, 139

    calendar events, 142

    reminders

        canceling, 141

        setting, 140-141

    time-related questions, 143

    timers, 141

Timer app, 228

timers

    canceling, 141

    pausing, 141

    setting, 141

    starting, 228

Time Travel feature, 51

Tip Calc (Calcbot app), 238

tips, calculating with Calcbot, 237-239

touchscreen, 4, 18

train stations, viewing information about, 158

translating languages, 240-243

transparency, reducing, 70

Turn Alerts option (Maps), 92

turn-by-turn directions. *See* directions

tweeting, 227

Twitter, 227

U

Uber app, 236-237

Uber cars, calling, 236-237

uninstalling Watch apps, 214

unlocking Apple Watch, 19

Upcoming Events (Calendar app), 85

updating Apple Watch, 27

Usage option (General Settings), 68

V

Verify option (Apple Pay), 190

viewing. *See* displaying

voice commands. *See* Siri

voicemail, 133-134

VoiceOver, 69

voice recognition. *See* Siri

volume controls, 130

W-X-Y-Z

walking directions. *See* directions

Wallet, 95-96

Watch apps, 211

    Activity app

        first-time setup, 13

        on iPhone, 199-200

        launching, 196

        Move Goal, 198

        navigating, 196-198

        personal information, 82

        settings, 82-84

    Alarm Clock, 230-231

    app icons, moving, 52-53

    Apple Pay, 95-96

    Apple Watch, 6

    automatic download, 216

    Calcbot, 237-239

    Calendar, 85-86, 233

    Camera, 225-226

    Clock, 86-87

    Contacts

        placing calls from, 132-133

        settings, 88

    Evernote, 247-248

    finding, 212

    Friends

        placing calls from, 135

        settings, 89-90

    Health

        choosing health sources, 205-206

        launching, 203-204

        navigating, 203-204

        viewing health data, 207-209

Instagram, 226-227

installing

    automatically, 216

    choosing apps to install, 214

    first-time setup, 11-13

    manually, 213

iTranslate, 240-243

launching with Siri, 146

Lose It!, 206

Mail, 90-91, 126-128

Maps, 149

    actions while navigating, 153

    directions, 151-157

    landmark information, 158

    launching, 150

    locations, 150-155

    Maps Glance, 150

    navigation taps, 153

    settings, 92

memory usage, 217-218

Messages

    composing messages from Friends list, 115

    composing new messages, 112-114

    handing off messages, 116-117

    handing off messages to iPhone or iMac, 116-117

    reading messages, 110-111

    settings, 92-93

    viewing sender details, 111

Music, 165

    accessing music source, 182

    creating playlists, 177-179

    finding music by album, 170-171

    finding music by artist, 167-169

finding music by playlist, 174

finding music by song name, 172-173

launching, 166

Music Glance, 184

My Music screen, 167

navigating, 166

pairing Bluetooth devices, 181-182

playback controls, 175-177

playing playlists, 182-184

sequence of playback, 176

settings, 94-95

synchronizing playlists, 179-180

notification settings, 216-217

Outlook, 245-247

Pandora, 224-225

Phone, 96-97, 130

Photos

creating Photo watch faces, 47-48

settings, 98

synchronizing photo albums, 41-45

PowerPoint, 249-250

rearranging app icons, 215

Remote, 222-223

running, 24

Siri. *See* Siri

Starbucks, 239-240

Stocks, 99

Stopwatch, 229

third-party Watch app settings, 102-103

Timer, 228

Twitter, 227

Uber, 236-237

uninstalling, 214

Wallet, 95

Weather, 100, 232

Workout, 200-203

ending workouts, 202-203

launching, 200

settings, 101

starting workouts, 201

viewing workout information, 202-203

World Clock, 229-230

Watch band release buttons, 5

watch faces, 29

changing watch face functionality, 49-51

choosing, 30-31

creating new version of existing watch face, 36-38

customizing, 31-36

deleting, 38-40

interacting with

complications, 20

Friends list, 25

Glances, 23

notifications, 21-22

running apps, 24

Siri, 26

Photo Album watch face, 40

choosing, 45-46

synchronizing photo albums, 41-45

Photo watch face, 40

creating, 47-48

synchronizing photo albums, 41-45

Time Lapse watch face, 48

Watch Orientation, 7, 67

weather
  asking Siri about, 144, 232
  Weather app, 100, 232
Weather app, 100, 232
Weekly Summary On/Off switch
  (Activity app), 84
words, translating, 240-243
Workout app
  ending workouts, 202-203
  launching, 200
  settings, 101
  starting workouts, 201
  viewing workout information,
    202-203
workouts
  ending, 202-203
  starting, 201
    manually, 201
    with Siri, 200
  viewing workout information,
    202-203
World Clock app, 229-230
Wrist Detection, 68
wrist, raising to activate Siri, 138

Zoom, 70

More Best-Selling **My** Books!

My
Windows 10

My
GoPro Hero Camera

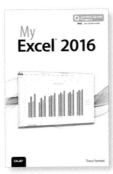

My
Excel 2016

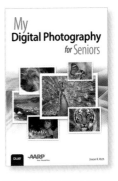

My
Digital Photography *for Seniors*

My
Office 2016 for Mac

My
OS X
EL CAPITAN EDITION

My
iPad
EIGHTH EDITION

My
iPhone
NINTH EDITION

Learning to use your smartphone, tablet, camera, game, or software has never been easier with the full-color My Series. You'll find simple, step-by-step instructions from our team of experienced authors. The organized, task-based format allows you to quickly and easily find exactly what you want to achieve.

Visit quepublishing.com/mybooks to learn more.

REGISTER THIS PRODUCT
SAVE 35%*
ON YOUR NEXT PURCHASE!

How to Register Your Product

- Go to quepublishing.com/register
- Sign in or create an account
- Enter ISBN: 10- or 13-digit ISBN that appears on the back cover of your product

Benefits of Registering

- Ability to download product updates
- Access to bonus chapters and workshop files
- A 35% coupon to be used on your next purchase – valid for 30 days

  To obtain your coupon, click on "Manage Codes" in the right column of your Account page
- Receive special offers on new editions and related Que products

Please note that the benefits for registering may vary by product. Benefits will be listed on your Account page under Registered Products.

We value and respect your privacy. Your email address will not be sold to any third party company.

* 35% discount code presented after product registration is valid on most print books, eBooks, and full-course videos sold on QuePublishing.com. Discount may not be combined with any other offer and is not redeemable for cash. Discount code expires after 30 days from the time of product registration. Offer subject to change.

31901056684808

quepublishing.com